PEARSON LONGMAN

CORNERSTONE

5

PEARSON English Learning System

Workbook

Anna Uhl Chamot

Jim Cummins

Sharroky Hollie

PEARSON

Upper Saddle River, New Jersey • Boston, Massachusetts • Chandler, Arizona • Glenview, Illinois

Pearson Longman Cornerstone 5
Workbook

PEARSON English Learning System

Staff credits: The people who made up the Cornerstone team, representing editorial,
production, design, manufacturing, and marketing, are John Ade, Rhea Banker,
Daniel Comstock, David Dickey, Gina DiLillo, Johnnie Farmer, Nancy Flaggman,
Charles Green, Karen Kawaguchi, Ed Lamprich, Niki Lee, Jaime Lieber,
Chris Leonowicz, Tara Maceyak, Linda Moser, Laurie Neaman, Leslie Patterson,
Sherri Pemberton, Diane Pinkley, Liza Pleva, Susan Saslow, Chris Siley, Loretta Steeves,
Kim Steiner, and Lauren Weidenman.
Text composition: The Quarasan Group, Inc.

ISBN-13: 978-1-4284-3488-2
ISBN-10: 1-4284-3488-7

Printed in the United States of America
1 2 3 4 5 6 7 8 9 10 V069 16 15 14 13 12

CONTENTS

CONTENTS

2

Name _____ Date _____

Key Words

Use with Student Book pages 8–9.

cooperate
bore
marvelous
grain
virtue
grateful

A. Choose the word that *best* completes each sentence. Write the word.

1. John was _____ for his home, his family, and his friends.

2. The farmer brought sacks of

   _____ for the horses.

3. George's mother said honesty is a _____ .

4. When we _____ , we finish our work quickly.

5. The orange trees _____ a lot of fruit.

6. We had a _____ time at the party!

B. Underline the key word in the row of letters. Then write a sentence for each word.

7. vreohgmarvelousnvrhg _____

8. ewruhfbhwgrainuwebhc _____

9. ewgvcooperatevbiur _____

10. fuebevgratefulruvb _____

11. ughouviuvbvirtuevnrenv _____

12. gugnvabborervnvbvm _____

Academic Words

Use with Student Book page 10.

assist
benefit
motive

A. **Choose the word that *best* completes each sentence. Write the word.**

1. He will _____ from his experiences at camp.

2. James will _____ his teacher with plans for the class party.

3. No one knew her _____ for the crime.

B. **Choose the word that best matches the meaning of the underlined words. Write the word.**

4. The high salary was her <u>reason</u> for joining the company.
_____

5. Please <u>help</u> him move the furniture. _____

6. The school hoped every student would <u>get something</u> from the new gym. _____

C. **Answer the questions.**

7. How do you **assist** your family at home?

_____

8. What are some **benefits** of having a summer job?

_____

9. What is your **motive** for studying hard?

_____

 **Use each academic word in a sentence. Share your sentences with a family member.**

4

Name _____ Date _____

Phonics: Long Vowel Pairs

Use with Student Book page 11.

> **Long vowel pairs** can be spelled in different ways. Some long vowel pairs are spelled with two vowels. Read each word. The first vowel is long. The second vowel is silent.

Long Vowel Pairs				
Long *a*	Long *e*	Long *i*	Long *o*	Long *u*
h<u>ay</u>	m<u>ea</u>t	p<u>ie</u>	f<u>oe</u>	s<u>ui</u>t
r<u>ai</u>n	f<u>ee</u>t		<u>oa</u>k	d<u>ue</u>

Find two words in each sentence that have long vowel pairs. Write the words. Circle the letters that make the long vowel pairs.

1. Did you eat a piece of fruit today?

_____   _____

2. We used to live on a main road.

_____   _____

3. He paid for the seeds with a $20 bill.

_____   _____

Write another word for each of the vowel pairs above. Share your work with a family member.

Comprehension: **The Three Gifts**

Use with Student Book pages 12–17.

Answer the questions about the reading.

Recall

1. Why was Jelani a good leader?

_____

2. What did Jelani want his children to do before they could go help people?

_____

3. How were the letters from Kofi's brothers and sisters alike?

_____

Comprehend

4. What were the problems in the villages that Kofi and Jelani visited?

_____

_____

Analyze

5. What did Kofi learn about helping people after visiting his siblings?

_____

_____

_____

Name _____ Date _____

Reader's Companion

Use with Student Book pages 12–17.

The Three Gifts

When Ada finished school, she went to other villages where she worked hard to help people. Ada's brothers and sisters admired her. She sent drawings of the school she helped to build. Ada wrote that it was a big job, but lots of fun.

One by one, Ada's brothers and sisters finished school. They all asked Jelani if they could go and help people. Jelani's eyes filled with joy each time, and he said, "Yes, you can help people."

In time, only the youngest son remained at home. His name was Kofi. Kofi loved to receive his siblings' letters. One brother helped dig wells for fresh water. Another brother helped farmers plant better crops. A sister helped a village hold an election to choose a better leader.

All of the letters were alike in one way. All of his brothers and sisters invited Kofi and Jelani to visit their villages.

Use What You Know

List three ways you can help others.

1. _____
2. _____
3. _____

Comprehension Check

What did Jelani's brothers and sisters do to help others? Underline where you found your answers.

MARK the TEXT

Reading Strategy

MARK the TEXT

Circle the names or descriptions of characters in the text.

Use the Strategy

How did identifying the characters and plot help you understand the story?

_____

_____

_____

Retell It!

Retell the passage from Kofi's point of view.

_____

_____

_____

_____

Reader's Response

Why do you think Ada and her brothers and sisters like to help others?

_____

_____

_____

Retell the passage to a family member.

Name _____ Date _____

Learning Strategies: Characters and Plot

Use with Student Book pages 18–19.

Read the passage. Answer the questions.

The Deal

Fall had arrived, and the corn was ready to be picked. Farmer Joe didn't know what to do. He had just broken his leg. "How am I going to harvest my crop?" he thought. Farmer Joe stood on his front porch and shook his head. "Hey there," said Jamal. "I'm your new neighbor." Farmer Joe waved. "Looks like your corn is ready," Jamal continued. Farmer Joe smiled and pointed to the cast on his leg. Jamal looked at the leg. Then he looked out at the cornfield and said, "I'll make a deal. I'll pick your corn, if you help me paint my house next spring." Farmer Joe was happy. He said, "You've got yourself a deal!"

1. Who are the characters? _____

2. Underline the main events in the passage.

3. What is the plot of the passage?

_____

_____

_____

Summarize the plot of this passage in your own words. Share your work with a family member.

Grammar: Future: *will* and *be going to*

Use with Student Book pages 20–21.

Review using *will* and *be going to* for talking about the **future**.

will + verb	I **will meet** her at the airport. She **will not be** here at 9:00.
be going to + verb	We**'re going to have** lunch after class. Sam **is not going to go** to the library today.

Use the words in parentheses to complete the sentences and questions. Use *will* or *be going to*. More than one answer may be possible.

Examples: I (eat) <u>am going to eat</u> breakfast in the morning.

I (eat) <u>will eat</u> breakfast in the morning.

1. The concert (end) _____ at 9 p.m.

2. There (is) _____ a party next Friday night.

3. (run) _____ you _____ in the marathon in May?

4. (ride) _____ you _____ your bicycle tomorrow?

5. He (stay) _____ home this weekend.

6. They (help) _____ clean up.

7. She (not miss) _____ the movie on Tuesday.

8. He (not fail) _____ the exam next week.

9. (go) When _____ they _____ on vacation?

10. (buy) What _____ you _____ for her birthday?

 **Write five sentences about things you plan to do in the next month. Share your ideas with a family member.**

Name _____ Date _____

Spelling: *ch* and *sh* Sounds

Use with Student Book pages 22–23.

A. Read each word. Pay attention to the sounds.

> ar<u>ch</u>es   <u>ch</u>ip   ou<u>ch</u>
> fi<u>sh</u>   <u>sh</u>ip   wi<u>sh</u>es

SPELLING TIP

When the consonant digraphs *ch* or *sh* are together in a word, they make one sound.

Choose four words. Write a sentence for each word.

1. _____

2. _____

3. _____

4. _____

B. Circle the words with the letters *ch* or *sh*. Write each word on the line. Then underline the consonant digraphs.

5. Which show do you like the best? _____

6. Our child likes to go fishing. _____

 Write a journal entry using at least five words that have the digraphs *ch* or *sh*.

_____

_____

_____

 Write six more words that have the digraphs *ch* or *sh*. Write a definition of each word in your own words. Share your work with a family member.

Writing: Describe a Future Event

Read the paragraph. Then read each question and circle the correct answer.

(1) My family is going to visit my grandmom in Chicago, Illinois. (2) We are going to leave a few days after Labor Day. (3) It is exciting to visit a big city. (4) My mom and grandmom and me will go to the stores downtown. (5) It is interesting see so many people in the shops. (6) You don't see that in my small town! (7) We will also visit the Museum of Science and Industry. (8) You can learn all about weather and the history of the railroad there. (9) After that, we are going to go to the Downtown Green Market. (10) The farmers there has all kinds of foods.

1. What is the BEST way to revise sentence 4?

   A I go with my mom and grandmom to the stores downtown.

   B I'll go with my mom and grandmom to the stores downtown.

   C My mom, grandmom, and me will go to the stores downtown.

   D No revision is needed.

2. What change, if any, should be made in sentence 5?

   A Change *see* to *to see*

   B Change *see* to *to seeing*

   C Change *see* to *seen*

   D Make no change

3. Which sentence could BEST be added after sentence 10?

   A Farmers live on farms.

   B My grandmother lives in Chicago.

   C The vegetables are very fresh.

   D Cowboys don't usually eat vegetables.

4. What change, if any, should be made in sentence 10?

   A Change *has* to *are*

   B Change *has* to *have*

   C Change *has* to *is*

   D Make no change

Name _____ Date _____

Key Words

Use with Student Book pages 24–25.

carry
scarce
share
peeked
cottage
charge

A. Choose the word that *best* completes each sentence. Write the word.

1. Will you help me _____ this stack of books?

2. There was enough food to _____ with everyone.

3. I _____ inside to see what was there.

4. The one-room _____ had a straw roof.

5. Water was _____ because it had not rained in months.

6. Watch the elephants _____ the lions.

B. Choose the word that *best* matches the meaning of the underlined words. Write the word.

7. She <u>took a secret look</u> while no one was around.

   _____

8. The roof of our <u>small house</u> leaks when it rains. _____

9. They burned dried grass because wood was <u>hard to find</u>.

   _____

10. Watch them <u>run quickly</u> into the pool! _____

11. Will you <u>give me part of</u> your sandwich? _____

Academic Words

Use with Student Book page 26.

| identify |
| occur |
| major |

A. Choose the word that *best* completes each sentence. Write the word.

1. When did the accident _____?

2. There was a _____ snow storm in Ohio last week.

3. He could not _____ the person in the photograph.

B. Match each word with its definition. Write the letter of the correct answer.

4. occur _____   **A** great in size or importance

5. identify _____   **B** to happen or take place

6. major _____   **C** to recognize or point out

C. Answer the questions.

7. What are three **major** events in your life?

_____

8. What types of flowers can you **identify**?

_____

9. What **occurs** every year on the fourth of July?

_____

Home-School Connection Write a sentence for each academic word. Share your sentences with a family member.

Name _____ Date _____

Word Study: Multiple-Meaning Words

Use with Student Book page 27.

Read each sentence. Put a check by the best meaning for the word in boldface type.

1. The sand felt hot and **dry**.

_____ **A** not wet, such as *a dry riverbed*

_____ **B** without enough oil, such as *dry skin*

2. The rising waters overran the **bank** of the canal.

_____ **A** business that holds people's money, such as *a savings bank*

_____ **B** steep side of a body of water, such as *a riverbank*

3. What was the first **state** in our country?

_____ **A** to say out loud or in writing, such as *state your name*

_____ **B** an area of land that is part of a larger country, such as *the state of New York*

4. Jason can **run** fast.

_____ **A** to try to be elected to an office

_____ **B** to move very quickly

5. John went to the **spring** to get water.

_____ **A** a place where water comes up from the ground

_____ **B** a coiled piece of metal

Home-School Connection Think of a word that has at least two different meanings. Write a sentence for each meaning. Share your sentences with a family member.

15

Comprehension: Stone Soup

Use with Student Book pages 28–33.

Answer the questions about the reading.

Recall

1. Why did John want to trade his big iron pot?

_____

2. What challenge did John face as he tried to trade the pot?

_____

3. What did John decide to do with the pot?

_____

Comprehend

4. How many items were added to the soup? What were they?

_____

_____

Analyze

5. What do you think John expected would happen when he began making the soup?

_____

_____

_____

Name _____ Date _____

Reader's Companion

Use with Student Book pages 28–33.

Stone Soup

One of John's favorite things was a big iron pot. The pot had once belonged to his mother.

As much as he loved the pot, John was hungry. He decided to trade the pot for something to eat.

"I'm sorry," said the farmer's wife from her cottage door. "Food is scarce these days. I only have enough for my own family."

"Thank you, anyway," John said. "I will carry my pot to the next village."

John walked many miles.

"May I trade this nice iron pot for something to eat?" he asked everyone he saw.

But the people in this village were just as poor and hungry as John was.

As John started to leave the village, he saw a smooth, round stone in the road. If only this stone were something good to eat, he thought.

Then John got an idea. He filled his iron pot with water. He gathered sticks and dry wood and then built a blazing fire all around his pot.

Reading Strategy

List three events in this passsage.

1. _____

2. _____

3. _____

Genre

A folktale is often a very old story. Underline a sentence that gives a clue that this is an old story.

Comprehension Check

Circle the text that tells why John wanted to trade his pot.

17

Use the Strategy

How did identifying events in the plot help you understand the story?

_____

_____

_____

Retell It!

Retell the passage as if you are the main character.

_____

_____

_____

_____

Reader's Response

What did you learn about helping others in this story?

_____

_____

_____

Retell the passage to a family member.

Name _____ Date _____

Learning Strategies: Events in a Plot
Use with Student Book pages 34–35.

Read the passage. Then write *E* for *Event* and *D* for *Detail*.

Stone Soup

John picked up his pot and headed home. Shortly after he started walking down the dirt road, he came across a perfectly round stone. "I wish this stone were something good to eat," he thought.

Then John got an idea.

He went back to the village, gathered up some wood, and began to build a fire. He dropped the stone into the pot.

Soon, a girl in a red dress came by with some potatoes. Then a boy came over and dropped some bright, orange carrots into the soup. As the vegetables began to cook, more people from the village noticed the smells. They started to bring more vegetables, meat, and spices.

John saw how hungry the villagers looked. "Will you stay and share this soup with me?" he asked.

1. _____ The stone was perfectly round.

2. _____ John dropped the stone in the pot.

3. _____ John gathered some wood and built a fire.

4. _____ The girl was wearing a red dress.

5. _____ The carrots were bright orange.

6. _____ People from the village brought vegetables, meat, and spices.

 **Have a family member read or tell you a story. (The family member can use his or her own language.) Talk about the events and details in the story.**

Grammar: Simple Past: Regular and *be* Verbs

Use with Student Book pages 36–37.

Review the **simple past** forms of verbs.

Regular verbs	save —➤ She saved all her money. cry —➤ The baby cried all day. play —➤ The kids played all afternoon. commit —➤ He committed the crime.
be verbs	am/is —➤ He was late for work. are —➤ They were ready to go.

Complete the sentences using the simple past form of the verb in parentheses.

Example: He (play) <u>played</u> tennis last weeked.

1. The play (start) _____ at 6:30.

2. There (is) _____ a plate of food on the table.

3. The accident (occur) _____ during a big storm.

4. I (am) _____ sick last week and couldn't go to class.

5. The boss (is not) _____ angry when I came to work late.

6. They (are) _____ always ready to help everyone.

7. She (try) _____ to play the piano.

8. The teacher (permit) _____ us to take the exam late.

9. The dog (stay) _____ in the same spot all day.

10. They (are not) _____ good at the game.

 **Write five sentences about things you did in the last week. Share your ideas with a family member.**

Name _____ Date _____

Spelling: Compound Words

Use with Student Book pages 38–39.

A. Use the two words to write a new word. The first one is done for you.

1. door   knob   __doorknob__

2. grand   mother   _____

3. under   ground   _____

4. house   boat   _____

5. sand   paper   _____

> **SPELLING TIP**
>
> When trying to spell compound words, look for a smaller word within the larger word.

B. Use each word to help you form a compound word. Some examples have more than one choice.

6. **day**   __daytime or Sunday__

7. **light**   _____

8. **water**   _____

9. **seat**   _____

✏️ Choose four of the words you wrote. Use each word in a sentence.

_____

_____

_____

_____

 **Home-School Connection** Write three more compound words. Circle the words that make up the compound words. Share your work with a family member.

Writing: Describe a Memorable Day

Read the paragraph. Then read each question and circle the correct answer.

(1) It was my first day at a new school. (2) I was entering mid-year, and I am afraid I couldn't make friends. (3) Ms. Ling, my teacher, introduced me to the class. (4) I was too nervous to speak. (5) Everybody stared at me as I took my seat. (6) At recess, I watched some girls playing softball. (7) They didn't notice me. (8) Suddenly, the ball rolled over to me. (9) I threw it back to them. (10) "Hey, you've got a great arm!" one of them said. (11) "You're Martina, right?" she asked. (12) I nodded. (13) "I'm Cassie," she said. (14) "Why don't you join us?" (15) I was so grateful to make friends on my very first day.

1. What change, if any, should be made in sentence 2?
   A Change *am* to *am feeling*
   B Change *am* to *feel*
   C Change *am* to *was*
   D Make no change

2. Which sentence could BEST be added after sentence 4?
   A I told them my name.
   B I just smiled.
   C I will miss my old school.
   D The teacher is nice.

3. What change, if any, should be made in sentence 11?
   A Change *?* to *!*
   B Change *You're* to *Your*
   C Change *Martina* to *martina*
   D Make no change

Name _____ Date _____

Key Words

Use with Student Book pages 40–41.

pilot
solo
mechanic
damage
skywrite
tradition

A. Choose the word that _best_ completes each sentence. Write the word.

1. A great way to wish someone happy birthday is to have a pilot _____ it!

2. The _____ flew the plane direct from New York to San Francisco.

3. It is a _____ in my family to eat turkey on Thanksgiving.

4. My mother is going to take our car to a _____ tomorrow to see what is wrong with it.

5. The pilot was nervous about making his first _____ flight.

6. If you _____ something in a store, you will have to pay for it.

B. Read each sentence. Circle the word that correctly completes the sentence.

7. Don't (pilot / damage) that statue when you move it.

8. He is going to (skywrite / solo) "I love you!" in the sky for his girlfriend's birthday.

9. The (pilot / mechanic) is going to repair the airplane engine.

10. James is excited to give his first (pilot / solo) performance.

11. Our family has a (damage / tradition) of eating pizza on Friday nights.

Academic Words

Use with Student Book page 42.

affected
establish
license

A. Choose the word that *best* completes each sentence. Write the word.

1. You need to get a _____ before you can drive a car.

2. His job was seriously _____ by the recent changes in the company.

3. If you want to _____ yourself in business, you need to work hard.

B. Read each pair of sentences. One sentence makes sense. The other is silly. Put a line through the sentence that is silly.

4. You need a license to eat soup.
You need a license to fly an airplane.

5. He wants to establish his own company.
He wants to establish his hairstyle.

6. Cold weather affected the crops in a bad way.
Cold weather affected the crops in a good way.

C. Answer the questions.

7. What are some things that you need a **license** to do?

_____

8. How are you **affected** by a sad movie?

_____

Copyright © by Pearson Education, Inc.

 Write a sentence for each academic word. Share your sentences with a family member.

Name _____   Date _____

Phonics: Short Vowels

Use with Student Book page 43.

| at | but | crop | fill | had | let | lift | not |
| ox | ~~pass~~ | rest | shut | then | trip | up | |

A. Sort the words according to their short vowel sounds.
One example has been done for you.

Short Vowels				
a	e	i	o	u
pass	_____	_____	_____	_____
_____	_____	_____	_____	_____
_____	_____	_____	_____	_____

B. Sort the words again. This time sort them according to their
spelling patterns. One example has been done for you.

Spelling Patterns			
VC	CVC	CVCC	CCVC
_____	_____	pass	_____
_____	_____	_____	_____
_____	_____	_____	_____

 **Home-School Connection** Add one more word to each column of both charts. Show your
work to a family member.

Comprehension: The Flying Schoolgirl

Use with Student Book pages 44–49.

Answer the questions about the reading.

Recall

1. Why did Katherine talk her parents into letting her take flying lessons?

_____

2. How old was Katherine when she obtained her pilot's license?

_____

3. How long did Stinson's career as a pilot last?

_____

Comprehend

4. How did Stinson stay involved in the war effort after being rejected from duty?

_____

_____

Analyze

5. How do you think Stinson's accomplishments helped the women of today?

_____

_____

_____

Name _____ Date _____

Reader's Companion

Use with Student Book pages 44–49.

The Flying Schoolgirl

Katherine Stinson obtained her pilot's license on July 24, 1912. She was just the fourth American woman to do so. Stinson found that she enjoyed flying so much that she gave up her plans for a musical career.

A year later, Stinson began performing as a stunt pilot. She traveled around the country. Because she looked so young, she was billed as "The Flying Schoolgirl." She was the first woman to perform the dangerous loop-the-loop trick. Over her career, she performed it over 500 times. And she did it in a plane she built herself! She was also the very first pilot to fly at night. Later, she was also the first pilot to skywrite at night. Using flares, she spelled out CAL in the skies over Los Angeles in 1915.

Reading Strategy

List three predictions you can make from the passage.

1. _____

2. _____

3. _____

Genre

Underline the important dates in the passage.

 MARK the TEXT

Comprehension Check

Circle the sentences that explained how Katherine Stinson got her nickname.

MARK the TEXT

Use the Strategy

How did previewing and predicting help you understand the passage?

_____

_____

_____

Retell It!

Retell the main points of the passage as if you were Stinson.

_____

_____

_____

_____

Reader's Response

Would you like to do the things that Katherine Stinson did? Why or why not?

_____

_____

_____

Home-School Connection

Retell the passage to a family member.

Name _____ Date _____

Learning Strategies: Preview and Predict

Use with Student Book pages 50–51.

Read the title and the first and last paragraphs of the passage. Answer the first question. Then read the entire passage and answer the second question.

A Good Solution

Tomorrow was Aimee's big tennis match. Everyone was sure Aimee would win. She was the school's best player.

"What's the matter, Aimee?" asked her coach. "You seem a little clumsy today. Did you hurt yourself?"

"Coach," she said, "I think it's my arm again."

The coach frowned. He knew Aimee had a sore arm. "Maybe Wanda should play tomorrow instead of you," he said.

"Wanda hasn't played all week," said Aimee. "She's at her grandmother's house."

"I have a plan," said the coach. "You go home and put ice on your arm. I'll call Wanda's grandmother."

1. What do you think the passage will be about?

_____

_____

2. Was your prediction correct? What does the passage tell you that you could not predict?

_____

_____

Preview a story by reading only the title and the first and last paragraphs. Share your predictions with a family member. Then read the entire story together to see if your prediction was correct.

Grammar: Past Irregular Verbs

Use with Student Book pages 52–53.

Review these **common irregular verbs**.

become → **became**	get → **got**	put → **put**
begin → **begun**	give → **gave**	set → **set**
break → **broke**	grow → **grew**	stand → **stood**
find → **found**	make → **made**	sing → **sang**

Write the correct past tense form of the verb in parentheses to complete each sentence.

Example: (make) My mother <u>made</u> a cake for my birthday.

1. (grow) My grandfather _____ orchids in his garden all his life.

2. (find) I _____ an antique ring on the train.

3. (begin) The performance _____ about half an hour ago.

4. (become) She _____ a nurse when she was 20 years old.

5. (put) Did you _____ the bread in the toaster?

6. (break) The glass _____ during the earthquake.

7. (give) Bobby _____ me a very nice present for my birthday.

8. (stand) She _____ behind me in the class photograph.

9. (sing) Who _____ that song?

10. (get) My dad _____ a speeding ticket for driving too fast.

 **Write five sentences about things you did today. Use the past tense of irregular verbs. Share your ideas with a family member.**

Name _____   Date _____

Spelling: Using a Dictionary

Use with Student Book pages 54–55.

Read this definition for the word *conduct*. Use the definition to answer the questions.

> con•duct[1] /kənˈdʌkt/ *v.* **1.** to control or manage **2.** to guide or lead **3.** *MUSIC* to lead (a musical group) **4.** to act in a certain way
> con•duct[2] /ˈkɑndʌkt/ *n.* **1.** the way a person or people act **2.** the act of controlling or managing

1. What parts of speech are shown in the definition for the word ***conduct***?

_____

2. What does the information between the slashes tell you?

_____

3. How many definitions are given for ***conduct*** when it is used as a noun?

_____

 Write two sentences. Use *conduct* as a verb in one sentence. Use *conduct* as a noun in the other sentence.

_____

_____

_____

 **Read the dictionary definitions of three words. Tell a family member what you learned.**

Writing: Describe a Person from History

Read the paragraph. Then read each question and circle the correct answer.

(1) William Clark was a famous American explorer. (2) In 1803, President Thomas Jefferson asked Clark and his friend, Meriwether Lewis, to take an important trip. (3) He wanted them to explore a large area of land called the Louisiana Purchase. (4) The United States had bought this land from the France.

(5) On their trip, Lewis and Clark met many Native American tribes. (6) Clark made drawings of the people he met. (7) Their trip was a great success. (8) President Jefferson pleased with their work. (9) He gives Clark a job working with the Native Americans in the Louisiana Territory. (10) He worked with them until his death in 1838.

1. What is the BEST way to revise sentence 4?

   A United States had bought this land from France.

   B The United States had bought this land from France.

   C This United States had bought land from that France.

   D No revision is needed.

2. What change, if any, should be made in sentence 8?

   A Change *pleased* to *is pleased*

   B Change *pleased* to *was pleased*

   C Change *pleased* to *pleases*

   D Make no change

3. What change, if any, should be made in sentence 9?

   A Change *Territory* to *territory*

   B Change *Native Americans* to *native americans*

   C Change *gives* to *gave*

   D Make no change

Name _____ Date _____

Review

Use with Student Book pages 2–55.

Answer the questions after reading Unit 1. You can go back and reread to help find the answers.

1. Which character do you think is the hero in *The Three Gifts*? Why?

_____

_____

_____

2. What are the three gifts in the story?

_____

_____

_____

3. Underline the words that show cause and effect in the passage.

> Jelani called out, "Stop everyone!" Jelani's advisors were soon teaching the others how to build a wood house. The people said, "You have helped us with this house, and now we can use these skills to build a whole village. One day, you will call on us, and we will return this favor."

4. In *Stone Soup,* what did John do when he found the stone in the road? Circle the letter of the correct answer.

    A He threw the stone into the river.

    B He got an idea to make stone soup.

    C He tried to trade the stone for food.

    D He put the stone in his pocket.

5. Name some of the items John and the villagers put in the soup.

_____

_____

6. What lesson did John teach the girl when he gave the stone to her?

_____

_____

_____

7. Make a connection to how you feel about Katherine Stinson after reading *The Flying Schoolgirl*. Describe what kind of person you think she was.

_____

_____

_____

8. Do you think it was easy or difficult to do what Katherine Stinson did in her lifetime? Why?

_____

_____

Home-School Connection   Tell a family member something new you learned in this unit.

Writing Workshop: Write a Descriptive Essay

Read the passage. Then read each question on the next page and circle the correct answer.

Camping by the Lake

(1) I like to go camping with my family at Lake Livingston. (2) The lake is so much fun. (3) In one part of the lake, people go swimming and enjoy the summer sun.

(4) As the sun sets, the sky are blue and orange, and looks beautiful over the water. (5) I can other hear campers talking and laughing nearby. (6) We cook dinner outdoors over a fire. (7) The fire makes a crackling sound, and feel nice and warm in the cool air.

(8) At night, we sleep in a tent. (9) I get inside my big, soft sleeping bag. (10) I can here the crickets singing a song. (11) I fall asleep and dream about another fun day.

1. Which sentence could BEST be added after sentence 3?

   A Swimming is a great way to exercise.

   B You should learn to swim if you don't know how.

   C In another part, people ride in boats or canoes.

   D The campground is about two hours from my house.

2. What change, if any, should be made in sentence 4?

   A Change *looks* to *look*

   B Change *are* to *is*

   C Change *over* to *top*

   D Make no change

3. What is the BEST way to revise sentence 5?

   A I can hear other campers talking and laughing nearby.

   B I can other hear campers talking and laughing nearby.

   C I can other hear nearby campers talking and laughing.

   D No revision is needed.

4. What change, if any, should be made in sentence 7?

   A Change *makes* to *make*

   B Change *air* to *airs*

   C Change *feel* to *feels*

   D Make no change

5. What change, if any, should be made in sentence 10?

   A Change *song* to *songs*

   B Change *here* to *to hear*

   C Change *singing* to *to sing*

   D Make no change

Name _____ Date _____

Fluency

Use with Student Book page 63.

How fast are you? Use a clock. Read the text about *The Three Gifts*. How long did it take you? Write your time in the chart. Read three times.

The Three Gifts tells the story of a caring and just	11
African leader named Jelani. He had seven children—	19
three daughters and four sons. After his daughter Ada	28
finished school, she went to villages to help people.	37
One by one, the children left their home to help people	48
in other villages, except for Kofi, the youngest son.	57
One day Jelani and Kofi decided to visit their family in	68
the different villages. In each village, people asked	76
them to help. Jelani and Kofi gave people sacks of grain,	87
clothes, and helped build wood houses. But when they	96
reached Ada's village, they saw a mudslide had ruined	105
the village. All the houses were gone. When all the	115
people from the other villages heard that Jelani and his	125
family needed help, they came to help rebuild Ada's	134
village to say thanks.	138

My Times

Learning Checklist

Check off what you have learned well. Review as needed.

Word Study and Phonics

☐ Long Vowel Pairs

☐ Multiple-Meaning Words

☐ Short Vowels

Strategies

☐ Identify Characters and Plot

☐ Identify Events in a Plot

☐ Preview and Predict

Grammar

☐ Future: *will* and *be going to*

☐ Simple Past: Regular and *be* Verbs

☐ Past Irregular Verbs

Writing

☐ Describe a Future Event

☐ Describe a Memorable Day

☐ Describe a Person from History

☐ Writing Workshop: Write a Descriptive Essay

Listening and Speaking

☐ Listening and Speaking Workshop: Give a Presentation

Name _____ Date _____

Test Preparation

Use with Student Book pages 64–65.

Read the selection. Then choose the correct words to fill in the blanks.

The Wildcats practiced hard for their first soccer game. They really worked hard to play as a team and _____1_____. Coach Wong and the girls were very excited about the game. But there was so much to do to get ready. The coach asked the girls to _____2_____ her. Donna and Mei made sure everyone had their uniforms and equipment. Wanda and Erin made sure the team had enough _____3_____ to drink and enough fruit snacks. Everyone arrived on time to the game. Afterwards, the girls _____4_____, "We are a great team!"

1.
  A fail
  B argue
  C cooperate
  D elect

2.
  F assist
  G carry
  H benefit
  J charge

3.
  A water
  B shoes
  C apples
  D crops

4.
  F told
  G wondered
  H asked
  J cheered

Read the selection. Then choose the correct words to answer the questions or complete the sentences.

Last Saturday was my piano recital. I was so nervous. I walked onto the stage and looked out at the audience. More than fifty people were sitting there, looking at me. I slowly walked to the piano and sat down. "Don't be nervous," I told myself. "Just play the music the same way that you practiced it." I don't remember what happened next. I just put my fingers on the piano and played. At the end of the song, I stood up and looked at the audience. They were clapping! I smiled and walked off the stage.

1. The main character walks slowly because she—
   A is nervous
   B plays the piano
   C practiced
   D sat down

2. What does the word <u>recital</u> mean? _____
   F Music
   G Practice
   H Instrument
   J Performanc

3. Why does the main character smile?
   A The audience looks at her.
   B She plays the piano.
   C The audience claps.
   D She's on the stage

4. The paragraph is mostly about—
   F a piano
   G a girl
   H a recital
   J a stage

Name _____ Date _____

Key Words

Use with Student Book pages 72–73.

A. **Choose the word that *best* completes each sentence. Write the word.**

1. He lives on a farm that raises _____.

2. The sheep eat grass in the _____ in the back.

3. Sarah wants a pet but she doesn't have time to _____ to one.

4. They act like brothers but they are not _____ at all.

5. We saw a big _____ of zebras when we went to the zoo.

6. You have to be strong to _____ a major illness.

B. **Write TRUE or FALSE.**

7. Cows are sometimes left in a pasture. _____

8. Friends are usually related. _____

9. A cowboy usually tends to cattle. _____

10. A dog is called a herd. _____

11. A person who survives is no longer alive. _____

Academic Words

Use with Student Book page 74.

aware
motivate
similar

A. Choose the word that *best* completes each sentence. Write the word.

1. He was _____ of the danger when he started down the hill.

2. Even though they are twins, they don't really look that _____.

3. Your teacher always tries to _____ you to study hard.

B. Underline the *academic word* in each row of letters. Then write a sentence for each word.

4. xclymotivatefrlvumzo _____

5. hlkywbqawaregkrmvjtx _____

6. sijfrwsimilarvpbhztmo _____

C. Answer the questions.

7. What **motivates** you to do something that you do?

_____

8. Who are you the most **similar** to in your family?

_____

9. Why is it important to be **aware** of the things going on around you?

_____

 Use each academic word in a sentence. Share your sentences with a family member.

Name _____ Date _____

Phonics: Vowel Pair *ea*

Use with Student Book page 75.

> The vowel pair *ea* can have the long *e* sound,
> as in *eat*, or the short *e* sound, as in *head*.

A. Read each word. Write whether the vowel pair *ea* has the
long *e* sound or the short *e* sound.

1. team _____

2. dead _____

3. lean _____

4. thread _____

5. steam _____

6. bread _____

B. Read each sentence. Find the word with the *ea* vowel pair.
Circle the word if it has the long *e* sound. Draw a box around
the word if it has the short *e* sound.

7. I ran so fast I couldn't catch my breath.

8. Having steak for dinner is a treat!

9. She used blue thread to sew her dress.

10. Each kid had a beach ball.

Write sentences for five words that have the *ea* vowel pair. Share
your sentences with a family member.

Comprehension: The Elephant Shepherd

Use with Student Book pages 76–79.

Answer the questions about the reading.

Recall

1. What was making the loud noise Ousmane heard while he was on the hill?

   _____

2. What will happen if the elephants stomp on the grass?

   _____

3. What was wrong with the elephant Amadou and his son found on the ground?

   _____

Comprehend

4. How did Ousmane feel about the elephant herd?

   _____

   _____

Analyze

5. What else might Ousmane and the villagers do to protect the elephants?

   _____

   _____

   _____

Name _____   Date _____

Reader's Companion

Use with Student Book pages 76–79.

The Elephant Shepherd

Early the next day, Ousmane and Amadou set out to find good grass for their cattle. They came across an elephant on the ground. They were shocked to see that the elephant's tusks had been sawed off.

* * * * * *

When he returned to school the following week, Ousmane decided to ask his teacher if his classmates could do something to protect the elephants. After school the next day, Ousmane and his classmates started to tell the other villagers why it was important to protect the elephants from poachers.

Use What You Know

List ways helping others can make you a hero.

1. _____

2. _____

3. _____

Genre: Short Story

Underline the words that show what the main character did in these excerpts from the story.

Reading Strategy

Circle the word that describes how Ousmane felt when he saw the elephant. Put a check next to the word if you felt the same way too.

Use the Strategy

Why is it helpful to make connections when you read?

_____

_____

_____

Retell It!

Retell what happens in the passage as if you are Ousmane talking to his teacher.

_____

_____

_____

_____

_____

Reader's Response

Have you ever felt like Ousmane about someone or something that was in danger? Write about the experience.

_____

_____

_____

Retell the passage to a family member.

Name _____ Date _____

Learning Strategies: Make Connections

Use with Student Book pages 80–81.

A. Read the passage. Answer the questions as they relate to your life.

The Class Project

Helen noticed how ugly the benches looked. Most of the paint had chipped or peeled away. Justine sat down as Helen looked at the bench across the path. That bench needed to be painted, too.

"Hi," said Justine.

Helen turned her head quickly. "I think I have an idea for the class project," she said. Last year, they planted trees on Main Street.

"What's your idea?" asked Justine.

"I think we should repaint all these park benches," Helen said. "I'll bet it has been years since they were last painted."

Justine nodded. "I think we've got ourselves a project!" she said. "Remember last year? We had the best time!"

1. What special place do you like to visit?

_____

_____

_____

2. What would you like to do to make that place better?

_____

_____

_____

Share your answers to the questions with a family member.

Grammar: Quotations

Use with Student Book pages 82–83.

Review the different uses of **quotations**.

| She looked at me and said, "I love you." |
| The doctor said, "**Y**ou are fine." |
| "**P**lease," said the guard, "**d**on't touch the art." |

Rewrite the sentences using proper capitalization and quotations.

Examples: hey she said come here

   "Hey," she said, "come here!"

1. you should not be in here he said _____

_____

2. she said please take a seat and be quiet _____

_____

3. if you run she said you may get hurt _____

_____

4. the man turned and shouted stop _____

_____

5. my name he said is Felix what's yours _____

_____

 Write five sentences using proper capitalization and quotations about things your family says. Share your ideas with a family member.

Name _____ Date _____

Spelling: /k/ Sound Spelled with the Letter c

Use with Student Book pages 84–85.

A. Read the words. Circle the words that begin with the /k/ sound spelled c.

1. class
2. cool
3. chase

4. chew
5. car
6. connect

> **SPELLING TIP**
>
> When the letter *c* is followed by *a, o,* or *u,* as in *cat, cone,* or *cub,* it stands for the sound /k/.

car	cat	cone	cub	cut

B. Read each clue. Write the word that matches the clue.

7. something you put ice cream in _____

8. your mom or dad drives this _____

9. you can do this with scissors _____

 Write a journal entry using at least four words with the */k/* sound spelled *c.*

_____

_____

_____

_____

 Think of five more words that have the */k/* sound spelled *c.* Write a sentence for each word. Share your work with a family member.

Writing: Write a Plot Summary

Read the paragraph. Then read each question. Circle the letter of the correct answer.

Bruno Silva

"The Lion and the Rabbit"
By Ed Young

(1) One night, Lion catches Rabbit. (2) Lion wants to eat Rabbit, but Rabbit trick Lion. (3) He tells Lion to look in the well. (4) Lion sees another lion in the well. (5) He shouts, "I is the king of the forest." (6) He hears his echo: "I am the king of the forest." (7) Lion is angry. (8) He jumps into the well. (9) Now Rabbit is safe.

---

1. What change, if any, should be made to sentence 2?
   A. Change *wants* to *want*
   B. Change *eat* to *ate*
   C. Change *trick* to *tricks*
   D. Make no change

2. What change, if any, should be made to sentence 5?
   A. Change *I* to *me*
   B. Change *is* to *am*
   C. Change *king* to *King*
   D. Make no change

3. What change, if any, should be made to sentence 6?
   A. Change *his* to *him*
   B. Change *hears* to *hear*
   C. Change *echo* to *ecco*
   D. Make no change

Name _____ Date _____

Key Words

Use with Student Book pages 86–87.

A. Choose the word that *best* completes each sentence. Write the word.

1. Doctors who work in unsafe places are

_____ .

2. Many _____ left the country during the war.

3. She had medical _____ so she could help the refugees.

4. Cooperation and _____ helped the people rebuild their village.

5. Aid workers _____ to help people in trouble.

6. People call 911 in an _____ .

B. Choose the word that *best* matches the meaning of the underlined words. Write the word.

7. With the right <u>instruction</u>, anyone can give first-aid treatment.

_____

8. The doctors will <u>come in and help</u> when disasters strike.

_____

9. Many <u>people who left their countries</u> came to the United States.

_____

Academic Words

Use with Student Book page 88.

> aid
> commit
> sufficient

A. Choose the word that *best* completes each sentence. Write the word.

1. You must _____ a lot of time to become good at sports.

2. He did not give _____ reason for being late and the coach got angry.

3. The volunteers gave a lot of _____ to the survivors of the earthquake.

B. Match each word with its definition. Write the letter of the correct answer.

4. commit _____   **A** to help or assist

5. sufficient _____   **B** plenty or enough

6. aid _____   **C** to pledge to do something

C. Answer the questions.

7. What is something you commit a lot of time to?

_____

8. Why might people sometimes need **aid**?

_____

9. What is a **sufficient** amount of time for you to sleep every night?

_____

 Write a sentence for each academic word. Share your sentences with a family member.

Name _____ Date _____

Phonics: Long Vowels with Silent e

Use with Student Book page 89.

> **Silent e Rule**
> When the first vowel (V) in a one-syllable word is followed by a consonant (C) and an e, the vowel is usually long. The final e is silent. Some verbs with a *v*, *m*, or *n* after the first vowel are exceptions to the rule.

A. Underline the words in the box that follow the CVCe pattern. Circle the words that are exceptions to the silent e rule.

bare	bride	cave	cone	dime	dove
glove	move	mule	one	pole	rake
some	state	theme	tune	were	

B. Choose five words with a long vowel and a silent e. Write a sentence for each word.

_____

_____

_____

_____

_____

Home-School Connection Write five more words with the CVCe pattern. Share your words with a family member.

Comprehension: Doctors Without Borders

Use with Student Book pages 90–93.

Answer the questions about the reading.

Recall

1. How long has Doctors Without Borders been helping people?

_____

2. How did Doctors Without Borders help after the tsunami in 2004?

_____

3. Why do refugees have to leave their homes?

_____

Comprehend

4. Besides medical help, what else does Doctors Without Borders provide?

_____

_____

Analyze

5. Why is this volunteer group called "Doctors Without Borders"?

_____

_____

_____

Name _____   Date _____

Reader's Companion

Use with Student Book pages 90–93.

Doctors Without Borders

In 2004 there was a tsunami, or tidal wave, in South Asia. The tsunami destroyed many towns. Many people were hurt or killed.

Doctors Without Borders worked for more than a year in countries that were hit by the tsunami. They gave people shots to make sure they did not get sick. The doctors gave people supplies like tents and clothing. They talked to people about what had happened. Sometimes just being there to listen to the victims helped the most.

Sometimes the volunteers help people in a town build new hospitals. That involves real teamwork!

Sometimes the best help the volunteers can give is training. It can be better for Doctors Without Borders to help train local doctors to take care of people after a crisis. The local doctors can give care to sick and hurt people after Doctors Without Borders leaves the area.

Use What You Know

List three things you already know about doctors.

1. _____

2. _____

3. _____

Genre

Underline two things Doctors Without Borders did after the tsunami.

MARK the TEXT

Comprehension Check

MARK the TEXT

Circle the part of the text that explains why training is important for Doctors Without Borders.

Use the Strategy

How did identifying the problem and solution help you understand the passage?

_____

_____

_____

Summarize It!

Summarize the passage for a partner.

_____

_____

_____

_____

Reader's Response

Would you like to volunteer for Doctors without Borders? Why or why not?

_____

_____

_____

Summarize the passage for a family member.

Name _____ Date _____

Learning Strategies: Problem and Solution

Use with Student Book pages 96–97.

Read the passage. Then answer the questions.

The Chiprock

The planet had become very cold. There was ice and snow everywhere. The Chiprock found it hard to grow their crops. They could not hunt for food because they could not run on the ice. The Chiprock could not even walk on it. Gunk, their leader, decided it was best to move underground.

Many of the Chiprock were unhappy about moving underground. After all, they had some luck growing crops indoors. In addition, Gunk's son and his friends were teaching the others to skate on the ice.

Gunk called a meeting of the tribe's leaders to discuss the issue. After many hours of debating and voting, they decided to stay above ground.

1. What are the problems in this passage?

_____

_____

2. How did the members of the tribe solve their problem?

_____

_____

Write at least three sentences about a character and a problem. Share your sentences with a family member.

Grammar: Adverbs of Frequency and Intensity

Use with Student Book pages 98–99.

Review these common **adverbs of frequency and intensity**.

He is **always** late for class.	They were **pretty** upset.
She **usually** has pasta for lunch.	She talked **really** fast.
I **rarely** go swimming.	He **almost** got hit by a car.
I **sometimes** go skiing.	We **barely** finished on time.

Choose an adverb of frequency or intensity from the box to complete the sentences. More than one answer may be possible.

always	sometimes	never	just	rarely
usually	pretty	almost	really	barely

Example: I <u>almost</u> missed my bus.

1. She _____ jogs in the mornings.

2. I think she's a _____ nice person.

3. It is _____ necessary to call the police.

4. Volunteers _____ try to help people after a disaster.

5. Do you _____ come to school by bus?

6. I _____ like to eat something sweet.

7. My boss _____ yells when he is angry.

8. A good coach _____ tries to encourage his team.

9. My parents _____ arrived home from Alaska.

10. That dog is _____ friendly most of the time.

 Write five sentences with adverbs of frequency and intenisty.
Share your ideas with a family member.

Spelling: Plural Nouns
Use with Student Book pages 100–101.

Use the correct form of the noun to complete each sentence.

1. We bought the children some new _____.
(toy/toys)

2. I went to the library to get some _____
(book/books)

3. Wooden _____ are hard to sit on. (bench/benches)

4. Dad ate both _____ of ice cream. (bowl/bowls)

5. I work for a _____ that makes cars.
(company/companies)

6. The price of _____ is high. (gas/gases)

7. All the _____ in town sell fresh bread. (bakery/
bakeries)

✏️ **Choose two of the word pairs in parentheses. Write a paragraph using both the singular and plural forms of the words.**

_____

_____

_____

_____

Home-School Connection

Write the plural form of three objects you see around you.
Show your work to a family member.

Writing: Write a Personal Message

Read the message. Then read each question and circle the correct answer.

Dear Sunita,

(1) It was great to hear from you! (2) I'm happy that you like your new school. (3) Are you really still wearing shorts? (4) That's hard to believe, since we have snow here in Chicago!

(5) You may have heard about our big storm. (6) The news isn't all bad, though. (7) Yes, we're going ski in Wisconsin next weekend. (8) I can't wait!

(9) Remember the dog show we went to last year? (10) They held them again this year. (11) Just about every dog in town was in the show. (12) I'm trying to talk my folks into getting me a dog!

(13) Write soon, and tell me all about Texas. (14) I miss you.

Your friend, Nestor

1. Which sentence could BEST be added after sentence 5?
   A How did you hear about it?
   B I think it's bad news.
   C It was very cold.
   D I like the snow.

2. What change, if any, should be made in sentence 7?
   A Change *ski* to *skiing*
   B Change *going* to *go to*
   C Change *next weekend* to *on next weekend*
   D Make no change

3. What change, if any, should be made in sentence 10?
   A Change *them* to *this*
   B Change *them* to *it*
   C Change *them* to *another*
   D Make no change

Name _____ Date _____

Key Words

Use with Student Book pages 102–103.

> eager
> pretended
> fastened
> clever
> punishment
> scattered

A. Choose the word that *best* completes each sentence. Write the word.

1. He _____ his seatbelt when he got in the car.

2. It takes a _____ person to solve these problems.

3. I am _____ to hear about the results of the competition.

4. The _____ for stealing is quite severe.

5. The wind _____ my papers all over the place.

6. When I was young, I always _____ to be a cowboy.

B. Read each sentence. Circle the word that correctly completes the sentence.

7. They (pretended / clever) they were older than they really are.

8. She (fastened / scattered) seeds all over the yard.

9. We were (punishment / eager) to begin our trip.

10. My mother (fastened / pretended) a ribbon on my dress.

11. The (pretended / punishment) for cheating was detention.

Academic Words

Use with Student Book page 104.

attach
challenge
secure

A. Choose the word that *best* completes each sentence. Write the word.

1. He worked hard to _____ the job.

2. Please _____ a photograph to your application.

3. The test was a real _____, but I think I passed.

B. Choose the word that best matches the meaning of the underlined words. Write the word.

4. It was a real <u>battle</u> for him to win the election.

_____

5. The teacher <u>fastens</u> a blue ribbon on the winner.

_____

6. She wants to <u>work hard to get</u> an A on the test.

_____

C. Answer the questions.

7. What are some things you might **attach** to your clothes?

_____

8. How can you **secure** an A on your next English test?

_____

 Use each academic word in a sentence. Share your sentences with a family member.

62

Name _____ Date _____

Word Study: Word Origins

Use with Student Book page 105.

> Some of the words you use every day come from other languages.

| canoe   chocolate   queen   tennis |

Read the words. Then read about the words. Match each word with its description.

1. The name of this female ruler comes from the German word *qino* and later the English word *cwene* which meant "woman."

_____

2. This word names a dessert or flavoring. It comes from *tchocoatl*, a word in Nahuatl, the language of the Aztecs. This group lived in Mexico.

_____

3. This word names a type of wooden dugout boat. The word is taken from *canaoua*, a word from the Arawak, a Native American group on the island of Haiti. Columbus introduced the word to Spain where it became the Spanish *canoa*.

_____

4. The name of this sport comes from the French word *tenez*, a form of the verb *tenir*. The meaning of *tenir* is "there you go." Players would say "tenez" when they hit the ball during a game.

_____

Copyright © by Pearson Education, Inc.

Think of five words that come from another language. (You may use your own language.) Look up the words in the dictionary to learn about their origins. Ask a family member to help you.

Comprehension:

The Origin of Fire/Water Spider Gets the Fire

Use with Student Book pages 106–113.

Answer the questions about the reading.

Recall

1. What did Fox have to do before the geese would teach him their cry?

_____

2. Why did Fox's wings suddenly stop working?

_____

3. How did Water Spider carry the fire back to the other animals?

_____

Comprehend

4. How did Fox use the piece of cedar bark that he secretly tied to his tail?

_____

_____

Analyze

5. What motivated all the animals to want to bring fire to the others?

_____

_____

_____

Name _____ Date _____

Reader's Companion

Use with Student Book pages 106–113.

"The Origin of Fire"

Fox ran and ran. Everywhere he went, Fox's tail set the bushes and trees along the side of the path on fire.

When Fox found Hawk, he gave the burning bark to the bird. Hawk flew high above the ground and scattered fire sparks everywhere. This is how fire came to the whole world.

"Water Spider Gets the Fire"

Water Spider spun a thread from her body and wove it into a bowl. Then she fastened the bowl on her back.

Water Spider ran on top of the water all the way to the island. Then she put one little burning coal in the bowl on her back. Water Spider ran on top of the water again to carry fire back to all the other animals.

Use What You Know

List the animals mentioned in these stories.

1. _____

2. _____

3. _____

Genre: Myth

Circle the words in the passages that help you understand that the passages are myths.

Comprehension Check

How did each hero secure fire? Underline the text where you found your answer.

Use the Strategy

How did comparing and contrasting help you understand the passages?

_____

_____

_____

Retell It!

Retell one of the stories as if you are the main character.

_____

_____

_____

_____

Reader's Response

Why do you think people still tell these kinds of old stories?

_____

_____

_____

Retell the passage to a family member.

Name _____ Date _____

Learning Strategies: Compare and Contrast

Use with Student Book pages 114–115.

Read the passage. Pay attention to things that are similar and different. Then answer the questions.

Training for the Big Race

My friends Maurice and Angelina are getting ready for the big race. They have been training for weeks. Maurice works out every morning for two hours. He likes to train before he goes to school. Angelina also trains for two hours every day. She likes to work out in the afternoon, after school. Angelina spends 30 minutes in the gym. Then she goes running for 45 minutes. Next, she swims for 30 minutes. Maurice also goes to the gym for 30 minutes. He runs for 45 minutes, too. He does not go swimming, though. He rides his bike instead. Both of my friends are working very hard. They can't wait for the big day!

1. How is Maurice's and Angelina's training similar?

_____

_____

2. How is their training different?

_____

_____

Compare and contrast two objects in your home. Share your work with a family member.

Grammar: Possessives

Use with Student Book pages 116–117.

Review the various types of **possessives.**

The girl**'s** book
The student**s'** books
Paul and Donna**'s** books
Jane's and Aron**'s** books
My, his, her, your, its, our, their books

Rewrite each phrase using the proper possessive.

Example: the dress of Sheila

<u>Sheila's dress</u>

1. the party of Adrian and the party of Alex

_____

2. the uncle of Robert _____

3. the house of Jon and Jason _____

4. the shoes of Maria _____

5. the bike of him _____

6. the food of them _____

7. the lights of car _____

8. the aunt of me _____

9. the bowl of it _____

10. the school of the students _____

 **Write five sentences about things you or your family possess. Share your ideas with a family member.**

Name _____ Date _____

Spelling: Words with Apostrophes

Use with Student Book pages 118–119.

do not can also be written as ***don't***
I <u>do not</u> want that. / I <u>don't</u> want that. * The apostrophe takes the place of the letter *o* in *not*.

SPELLING TIP

An **apostrophe** (') takes the place of letters left out in words like ***don't***.

Follow the model above. Join the words, leave out a letter and add an apostrophe to form contractions.

1. should not _____

2. it will _____

3. he is _____

4. are not _____

5. they are _____

6. can not _____

 Write a short paragraph using words with contractions.

_____

_____

_____

_____

 Write a paragraph that includes some of the contractions you studied. Circle the contractions. Share your work with a family member.

69

Writing: Write a Myth

Read the myth. Then read each question and circle the correct answer.

(1) In ancient Greece there lived a girl named Helena. (2) She was very good a weaver and made beautiful clothes. (3) In fact, she told people that in her clothes a woman would look more beautiful than the goddess Athena.

(4) When Athena heard this, she became very angry and go to visit the girl. (5) "I challenge you to a contest! (6) Helena's shop was in the city. (7) We will both weave a cloak and we'll see whose is the best!"

(8) Athena and the girl both began to weave. (9) Soon the young girl saw that Athena's cloak was far better than her own.

(10) "From now on," Athena said, "you will be an ugly insect. (11) You will weave a cocoon. (12) Only after you come out of the cocoon will you be beautiful."

(13) And with that, the girl turned into a caterpillar.

1. What change, if any, should be made in sentence 4?
    A Change *go* to *went*
    B Change *the girl* to *a girl*
    C Change *became* to *become*
    D Make no change

2. What is the BEST way to revise sentence 2?
    A She was a weaver very good and made beautiful clothes.
    B She was a very good weaver and made beautiful clothes.
    C She was very good a weaver and made a beautiful clothes.
    D No revision is needed.

3. Which sentence does NOT belong in this story?
    A Sentence 2
    B Sentence 6
    C Sentence 9
    D Sentence 11

Name _____ Date _____

Review

Use with Student Book pages 66–119.

Answer the questions after reading Unit 2. You can go back and reread to help find the answers.

1. In *The Elephant Shepherd*, suppose that Ousmane met one of the poachers. What do you think he would say?

_____

_____

2. Which sentence does NOT use a key word correctly? Circle the letter of the correct answer.

   A The two brothers look so different—I can't believe they're related.
   B Because of the war, there are many refugees.
   C We herd there was an emergency.
   D Animals need food and water to survive.

3. How did your prior knowledge about doctors help you understand *Doctors Without Borders*?

_____

_____

4. Which word has the same meaning as ***courageous***? Circle the letter of the correct answer.

   A weak   **C** afraid
   B brave   **D** clever

5. Go to the library or the Internet and find out what Doctors Without Borders is doing now. Describe some problems and solutions related to some of their recent work.

_____

_____

6. Think back to *The Origin of Fire* and *Water Spider Gets the Fire*. Which story did you like better? Why?

_____

_____

7. Which word has the same meaning as ***clever***? Circle the letter of the correct answer.

A desiring   **C** smart

B problem   **D** attached

8. Who are some real heroes in your life? Why?

_____

_____

 **Tell a family member something new you learned from this unit.**

Name _____ Date _____

Writing Workshop: Write a Story

Read the passage. Then read each question on the next page and circle the correct answer.

The Five-Dollar Hero

(1) Marcus was walking to school one rainy day. (2) A woman walking in front of him opened hers umbrella. (3) A strong wind came and the umbrella fell. (4) When the woman picked it up, something fell out of her bag.

(5) It was a five-dollar bill! (6) The woman didn't see it. (7) Marcus picked it up. (8) "What should I do?" he thought. (9) "Maybe she won't miss this money."

(10) Instead, Marcus called to the woman. (11) "Hey! You dropped something!" he yelled. (12) The woman stopped. (13) Marcus gave her the money.

(14) "Oh, thank you!" she said. (15) "I'm starting a new job today. (16) You're my hero!"

(17) Marcus smiled. (18) Being a hero was even better then getting five dollars.

1. What change, if any, should be made in sentence 2?
   A Change *woman* to *women*
   B Change *hers* to *her*
   C Change *him* to *his*
   D Make no change

2. What change, if any, should be made in sentence 6?
   A Change *see* to *saw*
   B Change *woman* to *women*
   C Change *it* to *them*
   D Make no change

3. What is the BEST way to combine sentences 12 and 13?
   A The woman stopped, and Marcus gave her the money.
   B The woman stopped, and gave the money Marcus.
   C The woman stopped, and her Marcus gave the money.
   D No revision is needed.

4. Which sentence could BEST be added after sentence 15?
   A A job is a great way to make extra money.
   B I found a job online.
   C I need this money for the bus.
   D I work 40 hours a week.

5. What change, if any, should be made in sentence 18?
   A Change *better* to *best*
   B Change *then* to *than*
   C Change *getting* to *got*
   D Make no change

Name _____ Date _____

Fluency

Use with Student Book page 127.

How fast are you? Use a clock. Read the text about *The Elephant Shepherd.* How long did it take you? Write your time in the chart. Read three times.

The Elephant Shepherd tells the story of a little boy named	11
Ousmane who was in charge of watching the cattle on the	22
savanna. One day a herd of elephants came to graze near the	34
cattle. Ousmane was excited. He loved watching the elephants.	43
Suddenly Ousmane's father, Amadou, appeared. He made the	51
elephants move away from his cattle. He explained to Ousmane	61
that elephants would stomp all over the grass that the cattle	72
need for food.	75
The next day the boy and his dad were looking for more grass	88
when they came across an elephant on the ground. Poachers had	99
sawed off the elephant's tusks to sell for money. Ousmane was	110
very sad. He wanted to protect the elephants. At school, he told his	123
teacher and his friends about the elephant. After school, he and	134
his classmates worked to protect elephants.	140

My Times

Learning Checklist

Check off what you have learned well. Review as needed.

Word Study and Phonics

☐ Vowel Pair *ea-*

☐ Long Vowels with Silent *e*

☐ Word Origins

Strategies

☐ Make Connections

☐ Identify Problems and Solutions

☐ Compare and Contrast

Grammar

☐ Quotations

☐ Adverbs of Frequency and Intensity

☐ Possessives

Writing

☐ Write a Dialogue

☐ Write a Personal Message

☐ Write a Myth

☐ Writing Workshop: Write a Story

Listening and Speaking

☐ Listening and Speaking Workshop: Perform a Skit

Name _____ Date _____

Test Preparation

Use with Student Book pages 128–129.

Read the selection. Then answer the questions.

1 Cows don't look alike to themselves. But they do look similar to us. How do you think ranchers tell their cows apart? They put brands on them! A brand is a special mark ranchers put on their animals to identify them. Brands show which ranchers own which cows. Today, ranchers brand their cows by putting tattoos on them.

2 The designs that ranchers use are interesting. Each rancher has his or her own brand. Some of the brands have been in the ranchers' families for a long time. Hernando Cortés brought branding from Spain to America in 1541.

1. Why are brands used for cows?
   A So ranchers can easily herd them
   B So ranchers know how old they are
   C So ranchers know how many they have
   D So ranchers can easily identify them

2. Where does a rancher work?
   F In an office
   G In a factory
   H In the country
   J In Spain

3. In paragraph 1, what does the word <u>similar</u> mean?
   A Different from
   B Interesting
   C Unlike
   D Almost the same as

4. What is paragraph 2 mainly about?
   F How ranchers brand their cattle
   G The travels of Hernando Cortés
   H Information about branding designs
   J Imports from Spain to the New World

Read the selection. Then answer the questions.

Cities today are usually hotter than the countryside. In summer, the temperature in cities is usually 6° to 8° higher than the temperature outside cities. Why is this? Cities have fewer plants. Plants help cool the air. Also, cities have many parking lots, roads, and buildings with dark roofs. These dark objects take in the heat of the sun. At the end of the day, the heat goes out of these objects slowly. The air gets hotter. This means that the biggest differences in temperature between the city and the countryside happen at night.

1. The paragraph mainly explains—
   A why cities have buildings with dark roofs
   B why cities have fewer plants
   C why the countryside isn't as hot as cities
   D why there is more sun in the city

2. Why is there a bigger difference in temperature at night?
   F Cities have fewer plants.
   G There's more sunshine in the city.
   H Nights are longer in the countryside.
   J Cities have more dark objects.

3. What might help keep cities from being hotter?
   A Taller buildings
   B More plants
   C Bigger parking lots
   D Darker roofs

4. In this paragraph, "these objects" refers to—
   F Plants in the city
   G Parking lots, roads, and roofs
   H Plants in the countryside
   J Temperatures

Name _____   Date _____

Key Words

Use with Student Book pages 136–137.

rule
colonies
Minutemen
militia
Redcoats

A. Choose the word that *best* completes each sentence. Write the word.

1. Many countries were once _____ of other countries.

2. The _____ fought the Redcoats during the American Revolution.

3. British soldiers during the revolutionary war were called _____.

4. A _____ is a small non-professional army.

5. The United States was under British _____ over two hundred years ago.

B. Write TRUE or FALSE.

6. Redcoats were American soldiers.   _____

7. Militia are usually made up of ordinary people.   _____

8. Minutemen were supposed to be ready instantly.   _____

9. The United States originally had thirteen colonies.   _____

10. A country under another country's rule is under its control.   _____

Academic Words

Use with Student Book page 138.

infer
initially
inspect

A. Choose the word that *best* completes each sentence. Write the word.

1. A mechanic needs to _____ our car.

2. You can _____ how someone feels by the sound of their voice.

3. _____, you need to write your name and the date on the test.

B. Underline the *academic word* in each row of letters. Then write a sentence for each word.

4. wginspectvctefrlvumxo_____

5. frqywbqawinferhmovjtx_____

6. zerjrwsimdinitiallytp_____

C. Answer the questions.

7. How can you **infer** what someone is feeling?

_____

8. Who should **inspect** the scene of a crime?

_____

9. What do you do **initially** when you wake up in the morning?

_____

Use each academic word in a sentence. Share your sentences with a family member.

Name _____ Date _____

Phonics: R-controlled *ar, or, ore*

Use with Student Book page 139.

> The letters **ar** usually have the vowel sound found in *arm*. The letters *or* and *ore* usually have the vowel sounds found in *torn*.

Read each row of words. Circle the two words that have the same vowel sound.

1.	bark	door	art
2.	important	crown	corner
3.	march	arm	more
4.	orange	order	harm
5.	horn	hard	horse
6.	chart	party	more
7.	farm	work	garden
8.	store	share	shore
9.	purpose	porch	story
10.	rather	farther	charm

Home-School Connection Write a poem using rhyming word pairs with the /ar/ sound in *arm* or the /or/, /ore/ sounds in *torn*. Share your poem with a family member.

81

Comprehension: The Real Soldier

Use with Student Book pages 140–145.

Answer the questions about the reading.

Recall

1. What was the purpose of the Minutemen?

   _____

2. Why didn't Jacob hide with Emily when the Redcoats came to their farm?

   _____

3. Why couldn't Jacob help the Minutemen fight the Redcoats?

   _____

Comprehend

4. How were the Minutemen effective during the fight for the colonies?

   _____

   _____

Analyze

5. Do you think the Redcoats knew that Jacob was not telling the truth?

   _____

   _____

   _____

Name _____   Date _____

Reader's Companion

Use with Student Book pages 140–145.

The Real Soldier

Jacob was getting some wood to bring into the house when his mother rushed into the barn.

"Redcoats are here," she whispered.

Jacob was scared. He wondered if the British soldiers knew that his father and the other farmers were Minutemen.

Emily was scared, too. She ran and hit in Star's stall. Jacob wanted to hide with her, but his mother needed him. Together they walked into the yard to face the British soldiers.

Jacob was relieved when he heard what the Redcoats wanted. This time, they only wanted food and supplies.

Jacob chose his words carefully. "My father has gone to the market," he said. "We don't have anything here." Jacob didn't tell the soldiers that the "market" was General Washington's camp!

Use What You Know

List three things you know about the Minutemen.

1. _____

2. _____

3. _____

Comprehension Check

Circle the text that shows what "Redcoats" means.

Reading Strategy

What inference can you make about why Jacob lied to the Redcoats? Underline where you found your answer in the text.

Use the Strategy

How did making inferences help you understand the passsage?

_____

_____

_____

Retell It!

Retell this passsage as if you are Jacob talking to his father.

_____

_____

_____

_____

Reader's Response

Do you think Jacob was a "real soldier"? Why or why not?

_____

_____

_____

Retell the passage to a family member.

Name _____ Date _____

Learning Strategies: Make Inferences

Use with Student Book pages 146–147.

Read the passage. Then answer the questions.

Feeding Time at the Zoo

It was 7:00 on Monday morning. All the animals were pacing back and forth in their cages. They always made a lot of noise when Janet came. It was almost as if they were happy to see her. Janet started cutting large slabs of meat. Mabel came over to watch. It was her first day on the job. "It's like this everyday," Janet said. "Same time, same place." Suddenly, there was a loud roar. "Oh dear," Mabel said. "I think Max is tired of waiting!" "Here," Janet said. "Throw this meat into his cage. Be careful, though. Breakfast is his favorite meal!"

1. Where are Janet and Mabel?

_____

_____

2. What are Janet and Mabel doing?

_____

_____

3. How do you know?

_____

_____

Have a family member tell or read you a story. (Your family member can use his or her own language.) Talk about the inferences you can make from the story.

85

Grammar: Necessity (*should, have to, must*)

Use with Student Book pages 148–149.

Review the different uses of *should, have to,* and *must.*

You **should** be on time.	You **have to** be on time.	You **must** be on time.

Complete the sentences with the correct form of *should, have to,* or *must*. More than one answer may be possible.

Examples: You <u>should</u> try to come to the show.

1. They _____ take the train to town.

2. You _____ make a card for her birthday.

3. She _____ try to be a better student.

4. You _____ litter or throw trash on the street.

5. Stay home. You _____ come to class today.

6. He _____ take the dog for a walk every afternoon.

7. We _____ do everything we can to save energy.

8. If you want to be a member of the team, you _____ wear the uniform.

9. You _____ have a ticket to see the concert.

10. You _____ feed animals in a zoo.

 **Home-School Connection** Write five sentences using *should, have to,* and *must*. Share your ideas with a family member.

Name _____ Date _____

Spelling: Words with *ght*

Use with Student Book pages 150–151.

Read each clue. Write the word that matches the clue.

bought	caught	daughter
eight	fought	light
night	right	straight
tight		

1. comes after the number *seven* _____

2. opposite of *left* _____

3. past tense of *buy* _____

4. comes after *day* _____

5. opposite of *curved* _____

6. what you get from the *sun* _____

7. past tense of *fight* _____

8. not loose _____

9. female child _____

10. past tense of *catch* _____

 Write a journal entry using at least three of the words in the box.

_____

_____

 Write sentences for five of the words in the box. Share your sentences with a family member.

Writing: Write a Review

Read the review. Then read each question and circle the correct answer.

(1) <u>Little House in the Big Woods</u>, by Laura Ingalls Wilder, is a really interesting book to read. (2) It tells about life in Wisconsin in the 1800s.

(3) I liked learning how Laura's family worked to get and find food. (4) Today we just go to the supermarket. (5) But Laura's family had to grow own vegetables and hunt wild animals in the woods. (6) Laura and her sister had to make their own cheese and butter. (7) Cheese and butter are not really that healthy.

(8) I also liked finding out what people did for fun before television and computers. (9) Laura's father played the fiddle, sang, and told wonderful stories.

(10) If you are looking for a good book to read you should try this one.

1. What change, if any, should be made in sentence 5?
    A Change *the woods* to *woods*
    B Change *had to* to *should*
    C Change *own* to *their own*
    D Make no change

2. What is the BEST way to revise sentence 10?
    A If you are looking, for a good book to read, you should try this one.
    B If you are looking for a good book to read, you should try this one.
    C If you are looking for a good book to read you should, try this one.
    D No revision is needed.

3. Which sentence does NOT belong in this story?
    A Sentence 2
    B Sentence 3
    C Sentence 7
    D Sentence 9

Name _____ Date _____

Key Words

Use with Student Book pages 152–153.

confidential
delegates
merchants
tailors
cobblestone
curious

A. Choose the word that *best* completes each sentence. Write the word.

1. I am _____ to find out what is in that box.

2. It is a good idea to keep your personal information _____ .

3. When the family went to the market, they bought things from the _____ .

4. The horses sometimes found it hard to walk on the _____ streets.

5. _____ from the new colonies attended the Constitutional Convention in 1787.

6. _____ work hard to make sure our suits fit well.

B. Underline the key word in each row of letters. Then write a sentence for each word.

7. sefdiucobblestonezook _____

8. wereialcuriouskaod _____

9. proxiconfidentialsamaip _____

10. quelivydelegatesslexif _____

Academic Words

Use with Student Book page 154.

> circumstances
>
> **period**
>
> physical

A. **Choose the word that *best* completes each sentence. Write the word.**

1. Big changes took place during that _____ in time.

2. There was a _____ change in his appearance after he got sick.

3. Do not make a decision until you know all the _____.

B. **Match each word with its definition. Write the letter of the correct answer.**

4. circumstances _____   **A** having to do with the body

5. physical _____   **B** conditions, details, and facts

6. period _____   **C** a length of time

C. **Answer the questions.**

7. What **period** in your life has been the happiest?

_____

8. What **physical** changes happen when people exercise?

_____

9. What **circumstances** make you smile?

_____

 Use each academic word in a sentence. Share your sentences with a family member.

Name _____ Date _____

Phonics: Consonant Digraphs *ch*, *sh*, and *th*

Use with Student Book page 155.

> The letters *ch*, *sh*, and *th* are called **consonant digraphs**.
> Each consonant digraph stands for one sound. The letters *ch*,
> *sh*, and *th* can be at the beginning, in the middle, or at the
> end of a word.

**Find the words with the letters *ch*, *sh*, or *th* in each sentence. Write
the words. Then underline *ch*, *sh*, or *th*.**

1. She likes to wear matching shoes and shirts.

_____

2. When I am thirsty, I drink chocolate milkshakes.

_____

3. Both merchants are selling shiny children's toys at the fair.

_____

4. I did the wash without my mother's help.

_____

5. If I shoot the ball to the moon, will you catch it?

_____

6. The girls chased seabirds at the seashore.

_____

 Think of five words that have the consonant digraphs *ch, sh,* or *th.*
Write the words. Then read them to a family member.

Comprehension: One Hot Summer in Philadelphia

Use with Student Book pages 156–159.

Answer the questions about the reading.

Recall

1. When and where was the Constitutional Convention held?

_____

2. Why were guards at the State House?

_____

3. Where did people get water in the 1780s?

_____

Comprehend

4. Why did more people die in the 1780s than today?

_____

_____

Analyze

5. How is the way people use water different today than it was in the 1780s?

_____

_____

_____

Name _____   Date _____

Reader's Companion

Use with Student Book pages 156–159.

One Hot Summer in Philadelphia

Water sometimes made people sick in the 1780s. People had no way of knowing if their drinking water was clean. To be safe, people didn't drink much plain water. They drank cider, milk, tea, and coffee. They could boil water for tea and coffee.

Houses did not have bathrooms. People used buckets to carry water from nearby wells to their houses. They filled washbowls and pitchers with water to clean their hands and faces. People didn't take baths very often. When they did, they would set a big wooden tub in front of the kitchen fire. After they filled the tub, a whole family would bathe in the same water. The person who went last didn't get very clean!

Like the well, the toilet was outside. It was in a separate building called an outhouse.

Use What You Know

List three ways life was different in the 1780s.

1. _____

2. _____

3. _____

Comprehension Check

Underline two problems people had with water in the 1780s.

MARK the TEXT

Reading Strategy

MARK the TEXT

Circle the main idea in each of the first two paragraphs.

93

Use the Strategy

How did identifying the main idea and details help you understand the passage?

_____

_____

_____

Summarize It!

Summarize the passage.

_____

_____

_____

_____

Reader's Response

What would you have done about one of the challenges you faced if you lived in Philadelphia in the 1780s?

_____

_____

_____

Summarize the passage for a family member.

Name _____ Date _____

Learning Strategies: Main Idea and Details

Use with Student Book pages 160–161.

Read the passage. Circle the main idea. Underline three details.

The Summer Holidays

Summer finally arrived. The Holden family rented a beach house for the month of July. Mr. Holden was really excited because the house was bigger than the one they rented last year. There was enough room in the garage for all of his fishing tackle. He could even fit a boat in there! He was really looking forward to taking his son, Jimmy, deep-sea fishing.

After the family unpacked, they decided to rent a boat. They went to the boat rental place in town that was near the dock. The salesperson asked Mr. Holden what kind of boat he wanted.

"The biggest one you have," Mr. Holden replied. "Make sure the motor works! It would be great to have a refrigerator, too."

"I want a place to put my new fishing tackle," said Jimmy.

Mrs. Holden, Emma, and Ann didn't really care about the boat. They were more interested in renting some blue bikes and exploring shops along the boardwalk. They wanted Jimmy and Mr. Holden to hurry up. They got tired of waiting, so while Jimmy and Mr. Holden spoke with the salesperson, they went to the bike rental shop.

Home-School Connection Have a family member tell or read you a story. (Your family member can use his or her own language.) Identify the main idea and at least one detail in the story.

95

Grammar: Nouns

Use with Student Book pages 162–163.

Review the **singular and plural forms** of some common nouns.

bird ⟶ bird**s** spy ⟶ spi**es** potato ⟶ potato**es** wolf ⟶ wol**ves**
man ⟶ men foot ⟶ feet child ⟶ children

Complete the sentences using the correct singular or plural form of the word in parentheses.

Example: The (bird) <u>birds</u> live up in the trees.

1. The (shirt) _____ are all on sale.

2. The (child) _____ visit their grandmother every week.

3. A (man) _____ from the store called me yesterday.

4. My (foot) _____ are very painful after the race.

5. There are some (tomato) _____ on the table.

6. A (group) _____ of children crossed the street together.

7. There were three (team) _____ in the competition.

8. The teacher asked a (student) _____ to read aloud.

9. It took three (company) _____ to create this new car.

10. There is a lot of (proof) _____ against him.

 **Home-School Connection** Write five sentences about nouns that you use every day. Share your ideas with a family member.

Name _____ Date _____

Spelling: Endings -*le*

Use with Student Book pages 164–165.

Read each clue. Then complete the words.

1. something used to sew cloth   need _____

2. opposite of big   lit _____

3. many of us   peo _____

4. a crossword   puz _____

5. not doing anything   id _____

6. something to carry water in   bot _____

7. can do something   ab _____

8. to break into little pieces   crum _____

9. mix up a deck of cards   shuf _____

10. it helps you hold something   han _____

11. holds paper together   stap _____

 Write a message to a friend. Use at least three words with -*le* endings.

_____

_____

 **Think of five more words with -*le* endings. Write your own clue for each word. Share your work with a family member.**

Writing: Write a Persuasive Article

Use with Student Book pages 164–165.

Read the article. Then read each question and circle the correct answer.

(1) When you walk the streets of Philadelphia, you know you are in the birthplace of America. (2) You can almost feel the presence of people such as Benjamin Franklin Thomas Jefferson and Betsy Ross. (3) Congress met here during the Revolutionary War. (4) Afterward, it was the capital of the country from 1790 to 1800. (5) So if you're interested in American history, there is no better place to go!

(6) At Independence Hall start your visit. (7) This is where a group of men, including Jefferson and Franklin, worked on the Declaration of Independence in 1776. (8) Then cross the street to see the world famous Liberty Bell. (9) The streets in Philadelphia are not very wide. (10) When the Declaration of Independence was read for the first time, this bell called citizens to Independence Hall.

1. What change, if any, should be made in sentence 2?

    A Add commas after *Franklin* and *Jefferson*

    B Add *and* between *Franklin* and *Thomas*

    C Change *people* to *peoples*

    D Make no change

2. What is the BEST way to revise sentence 6?

    A To start your visit, Independence Hall.

    B At Independence Hall you can start your visit.

    C Start your visit at Independence Hall.

    D No revision is needed.

3. Which sentence does NOT belong in this story?

    A Sentence 3

    B Sentence 7

    C Sentence 8

    D Sentence 9

Name _____ Date _____

Key Words

Use with Student Book pages 166–167.

statesman
federal
liberty
surrender
veteran
republic

A. Choose the word that *best* completes each sentence. Write the word.

1. A _____ can take pride in having fought for our country's ideals.

2. Most decisions about education are made by individual states rather than the _____ government.

3. In a _____, the government is elected by the people.

4. A good _____ will work hard to support the government and uphold its principles.

5. George Washington led the final battle that caused the British army to _____.

6. The United States fought to gain _____ from Great Britain.

B. Write TRUE or FALSE.

7. After an army surrenders, they can celebrate their victory.   _____

8. In the United States, some government powers are federal and others are granted to the states.   _____

9. Citizens in a republic have no say in their government.   _____

10. Veterans are people who have never served in the military.   _____

11. People with liberty are free.   _____

12. A statesman might offer good advice to government leaders.   _____

99

Academic Words

Use with Student Book page 168.

cultures
expanded
impose

A. **Choose the word that *best* completes each sentence. Write the word.**

1. The company _____ over the years and is now one of the biggest in the world.

2. Please do not _____ your opinions on me!

3. Asia is full of a variety of interesting _____.

B. **Choose the word that best matches the meaning of the underlined words. Write the word.**

4. The <u>lifestyles and traditions</u> of the people from that region are quite interesting. _____

5. He always <u>forces me to accept</u> his ideas. _____

6. The area of their farm <u>grew</u> tens times in the past five years.

_____

C. **Answer the questions.**

7. What are interesting things about American **culture**?

_____

8. How would you try to **impose** your ideas on someone else?

_____

9. What have you seen **expand** in the last few years?

_____

 **Write a new question for each academic word. Try to answer your question. Then show your work to a family member.**

Name _____ Date _____

Word Study: Synonyms and Antonyms

Use with Student Book page 169.

> **Synonyms** are words that have the same or similar meanings.
>
> **Antonyms** are words that have opposite meanings.

A. Match each word with its antonym. Write the letter of the correct answer.

1. huge   _____   **A** weak

2. mean   _____   **B** old

3. light   _____   **C** tiny

4. strong   _____   **D** nice

5. young   _____   **E** dark

B. Read each word. Then draw a box around its synonym.

6. remove   take off / stick to

7. close   open / shut

8. healthy   ill / well

9. leave   go away / stay

10. begin   start / end

Home-School Connection

Think of synonyms and antonyms for these words: *short, wet, freezing, soft, furry*, and *sad*. Show your words to a family member.

Comprehension: One Out of Many

Use with Student Book pages 170–177.

Answer the questions about the reading.

Recall

1. When did the Constitutional Convention end?

_____

2. What was the new government called?

_____

3. What are the three branches of the government?

_____

Comprehend

4. Why does the president have a four-year term in office?

_____

_____

Analyze

5. Why do you think it was so important to the leaders of the
Constitutional Convention to limit the government's powers?

_____

_____

_____

Name _____ Date _____

Reader's Companion

Use with Student Book pages 170–177.

One Out of Many

Franklin: Yes. People are afraid of government. They think it will take away their liberty.

Ned: We don't want that!

Bob: Make the government weak!

Franklin: What if we have to fight the British again?

Bob: Didn't they surrender?

Washington: Yes. But they might come back.

Ned: We just need a strong army then.

Franklin: Armies cost money. Yesterday, I saw an army veteran in great need. We must take care of the soldiers who fought in the war. France gave us a loan. We should pay them back. Where will we get the money?

Bob: Oh. Is that the only problem?

Franklin: No! There are many things to figure out. But first, we need a strong federal government.

Washington: But not so strong we lose our freedom. Understand?

Use What You Know

List three fears people had about government in 1787.

1. _____

2. _____

3. _____

Comprehension Check

Circle the text that shows what Franklin believes the United States needs.

MARK the TEXT

Reading Strategy

MARK the TEXT

Underline a part of the passage that states something you already know about.

_____

_____

_____

_____

Use the Strategy

How did using prior knowledge help you understand the passsage?

_____

_____

_____

Retell It!

Retell this passsage as if you are one of the characters.

_____

_____

_____

_____

Reader's Response

Why do you think it was so difficult to write the U.S. Constitution?

_____

_____

_____

Home-School Connection   **Summarize the main points of the passage for a family member.**

Name _____ Date _____

Learning Strategies: Use Prior Knowledge

Use with Student Book pages 178–179.

Read the passage. Answer the questions.

What Do Nurses Do?

Nurses work hard to keep people healthy. They keep an eye on patients' temperatures, blood pressures, and vital signs. Nurses work in many different places. Some nurses work in doctors' offices. Other nurses work in hospitals. Some of them even work in the operating room.

Nurses work with both patients and doctors to make sure patients get the best care. They teach patients about their conditions and how to take care of themselves. They tell the doctors if the patient is having trouble with medication or medical equipment. They call the doctor right away if the patient has a life-threatening condition. They are often the first people an accident victim sees in the emergency room.

1. Describe something you knew about nurses before you read this passage.

_____

_____

_____

2. Describe something you learned about nurses from reading this passage.

_____

_____

_____

Copyright © by Pearson Education, Inc.

Share what you have learned about Doctors Without Borders with a family member.

105

Grammar: Compound Sentences

Use with Student Book pages 180–181.

Review these common types of **compound sentences**.

> The sky was blue, and the sun was bright.
> It was very early, and the air was cold.
> Yang brought a ball, but forgot his glove.
> We can go see a movie, or we can go ice skating.

Use the connecting words *and, but,* **or** *or* **to combine the sentences.**

Examples: She waited for an hour. The bus didn't come.

<u>She waited for an hour, but the bus didn't come.</u>

1. He wanted to be an actor. Now he is famous.

_____

2. She's cheerful. She's a very nice person.

_____

3. It was late. I was still waiting for him to call.

_____

4. I want to be a doctor. I want to be a veterinarian.

_____

5. It's a perfect day. We're going to go swimming.

_____

 **Write five compound sentences about things you noticed today. Share your ideas with a family member.**

Name _____   Date _____

Spelling: Spelling *i* and *e* Together

Use with Student Book pages 182–183.

A. Write the word that *best* fits each clue.

ceiling	fried	friend
neighbor	receiving	tie

1. the top of a room _____

2. someone you work and play with

_____

3. a person who lives next door _____

4. something you do to your shoelaces _____

5. giving is better than _____

6. some of your favourite foods are cooked this way

_____

 Write a paragraph using some of the words in the box.

_____

_____

_____

Home-School Connection   Write five more words that have the letters *i* and *e* together. Explain the Spelling Tip to a family member.

Writing: Write a Persuasive Poster

Read the poster. Then read each question and circle the correct answer.

(1) MIAMI, FLORIDA – YOUR NEW HOMETOWN!

RECREATION

(2) Miami has miles and miles of beaches and you can go swimming even in the winter!

GREAT ATTRACTIONS

(3) Everglades National Park is only one hour's drive away. You can go hiking, see amazing bird life, and take photos of alligators!

SUN! SUN! SUN!

(4) The weather is warm in miami all year round. (5) Throw your winter coats away!

(6) MIAMI, FLORIDA HAS IT ALL!

1. What change, if any, should be made in sentence 2?
   A Change *winter* to *Winter*
   B Add a comma after *beaches*
   C Change *beaches* to *beachs*
   D Make no change

2. What change, if any, should be made in sentence 4?
   A Change *warm* to *warmest*
   B Change *miami* to *Miami*
   C Change *in* to *on*
   D Make no change

3. Which sentence is NOT necessary in this poster?
   A Sentence 2
   B Sentence 3
   C Sentence 4
   D Sentence 5

Copyright © by Pearson Education, Inc.

Name _____ Date _____

Review

For use with Student Book pages 130–183.

Answer the questions after reading Unit 3. You can go back and reread to help find the answers.

1. What does the title *The Real Soldier* mean? Explain.

_____

_____

2. What is the meaning of the term *Minutemen*? Circle the letter of the correct answer.

    A men who had no patience for their rulers

    B men who could deliver messages quickly

    C men who only had short meetings during the war

    D men who had to be ready to act as soldiers anytime

3. Complete a 5 W Chart for *The Real Soldier.* Have a partner help you write answers to your questions.

5 W	Questions	Answers
Who?		
What?		
Where?		
When?		
Why?		

4. How was the important event described in *One Hot Summer in Philadelphia*? Circle the letter of the correct answer.

    A the Constitutional Convention   **C** the American Revolution

    B the Declaration of Independence   **D** the Civil War

5. What kinds of people lived and worked in Philadelphia in 1787?

_____

_____

6. List the delegates to the Constitutional Convention mentioned in *One Out of Many.*

_____

_____

7. Why did leaders in the United States hold a Constitutional Convention in 1787?

_____

_____

8. Americans elect officials to:

    A rule over them   **C** change the laws

    B represent them in government   **D** start wars with other countries

Home-School Connection   Tell a family member something new you learned in this unit.

Name _____ Date _____

Writing Workshop: Write a Persuasive Essay

Read the passage. Then read each question on the next page and circle the correct answer.

Let's Make a Bike-Friendly Town

(1) Many people ride bikes in our town, but it is difficult. (2) If we had bike lanes on our roads, cycling would be easier and safer. (3) Let's ask the mayor to make bike lanes for cyclists.

(4) Without bike lanes, bikes and cars are always try to share the road. (5) Sometimes there are accidents between cars and bikes. (6) With bike lanes, cyclists have its own space, and drivers can remember we are there.

(7) If cycling becomes the easier, maybe more people will ride bikes instead of driving. (8) You can buy a used bike online. (9) If more people ride bikes, there will be less pollution, to.

(10) Please write a letter to the mayor's office. (11) Let's ask her to make bike lanes. (12) It's good for everyone in our town.

1. What change, if any, should be made in sentence 4?

   A Change *are* to *have*

   B Change *to share* to *shared*

   C Change *try* to *trying*

   D Make no change

2. What change, if any, should be made in sentence 6?

   A Change *its* to *it's*

   B Change *its* to *their*

   C Change *its* to *theirs*

   D Make no change

3. What is the BEST way to revise sentence 7?

   A If cycling becomes the easier, maybe more person will ride bikes instead of driving.

   B If cycling becomes the easier, maybe more people will ride bikes instead driving.

   C If cycling becomes easier, maybe more people will ride bikes instead of driving.

   D No revision is needed.

4. What change, if any, should be made in sentence 9?

   A Change *less* to *least*

   B Change *to* to *too*

   C Change *will* to *is*

   D Make no change

5. Which sentence does NOT belong in this story?

   A Sentence 2

   B Sentence 7

   C Sentence 8

   D Sentence 10

Name _____   Date _____

Fluency

Use with Student Book page 191.

How fast are you? Use a clock. Read the text about *One Hot Summer in Philadelphia*. How long did it take you? Write your time in the chart. Read three times.

One Hot Summer in Philadelphia describes how people lived in the	11
1780s at the time of the First Constitutional Convention in the city.	23
Life was much harder than it is today. There were no trains or planes	37
for people to use to get to the Convention. There was no air	50
conditioning for the people dressed in hot, formal clothes. The State	61
House meetings were confidential, and so the doors and windows	71
were kept closed. When delegates got sick from the heat, people	82
called the doctor, but it wasn't common for people to go to doctors	95
like they do today. People had herbal teas and a few medicines from	108
plants. They drank milk, cider, tea and coffee because their drinking	119
water was not always safe. People didn't take baths often. Toilets	130
were outside the houses. Life was hard, but people from all over the	143
world came to live in Philadelphia.	149

My Times

Learning Checklist

Check off what you have learned well. Review as needed.

Word Study and Phonics

☐ R-controlled: *ar, or, ore*

☐ Consonant Digraphs: *ch, sh*, and *th*

☐ Synonyms and Antonyms

Strategies

☐ Make Inferences

☐ Identify Main Idea and Details

☐ Use Prior Knowledge

☐ Use a KWL Chart

Grammar

☐ Necessity: *should, have to, must*

☐ Nouns

☐ Compound Sentences

Writing

☐ Write a Review

☐ Write a Persuasive Article

☐ Write a Persuasive Poster

☐ Writing Workshop: Write a Persuasive Essay

Listening and Speaking

☐ Listening and Speaking Workshop: Give a Speech

Name _____ Date _____

Test Preparation

Use with Student Book pages 192–193.

Read the selection. Then choose the correct words to fill in the blanks.

There was once an armadillo who loved the sound of ___1___. He decided he wanted to learn to sing. He asked the frogs, the crickets, and the birds in the forest if they would teach him to sing. They all said the same thing, "No, silly! Armadillos don't sing." The armadillo was very ___2___. Why didn't the animals want to teach him to sing?

Then one day, an old man came walking in the ___3___. The armadillo asked the old man if he could teach him how to sing. The old man picked up a stick and tapped the armadillo on its ___4___. The shell-tapping made beautiful music! Soon all the animals in the forest came to listen to the old man and the armadillo make their beautiful songs.

1.
- **A** driving
- **B** singing
- **C** reading
- **D** fishing

2.
- **F** unhappy
- **G** joyful
- **H** athletic
- **J** musical

3.
- **A** forest
- **B** house
- **C** school
- **D** ocean

4.
- **F** foot
- **G** head
- **H** shell
- **J** doo

Read the selection. Then choose the correct words to fill in the blanks.

A long time ago, Wind and Thunder were fighting. "The green earth needs me more than you," said Wind. "No, I am more ___1___ for the earth," said Thunder.

"I am stronger," said Wind. Wind blew hard to show its ___2___. The Thunder got angry. It made a loud noise and went far away from the Wind.

"I can work alone," Wind thought. "I can make the tall grass grow by myself." So Wind blew and blew. But no grass grew. Slowly the earth changed from green to brown.

Wind went to Thunder and said, "The earth needs both of us. I am sorry." Thunder made a noise. The noise grew louder and louder. Then ___3___ fell on the earth.

Soon the earth was green, and Wind was happy to blow the tall grass again. From that day, Wind and Thunder always worked ___4___.

1.
  A important
  B interesting
  C beautiful
  D better

2.
  F interest
  G beauty
  H peace
  J power

3.
  A light
  B snow
  C leaves
  D rain

4.
  F alone
  G hard
  H together
  J slowly

Name _____ Date _____

Key Words

Use with Student Book pages 200–201.

biome
tundra
equator
desert
tropical
grasslands
ocean

A. Choose the word that *best* completes each sentence. Write the word.

1. An area that is very hot and very wet is

   said to be _____ .

2. The soil in the _____ is
   frozen most of the year.

3. The imaginary line around the middle of Earth is the

   _____ .

4. An area of land that receives very little rain is a

   _____ .

5. The great quantity of salt water that covers most of Earth is the

   _____ .

6. A large area characterized by specific plants and animals is a

   _____ .

7. _____ are large areas where there are many
   grasses, but few trees.

Academic Words

Use with Student Book page 202.

adapted

label

migrate

A. Choose the word that *best* completes each sentence. Write the word.

1. Birds are one of many animals that _____ as the seasons change each year.

2. We _____ biomes based on the weather and the plants and animals that live there.

3. I _____ to a new school when we moved.

B. Match each word with its definition. Write the letter of the correct answer.

4. adapted _____   **A** changed to fit a new situation

5. label _____   **B** to move from one place to another

6. migrate _____   **C** describe a person or a thing

C. Answer the questions.

7. What things have you **adapted** to in your life?

_____

8. How do you **label** a KWL chart?

_____

9. What things might motivate people to **migrate** from one country to another?

_____

Use each academic word in a sentence. Share your sentences with a family member.

Name _____ Date _____

Phonics: Final *s* sound: *z, s, iz*

Use with Student Book page 203.

A final *s* can be pronounced like *s*, *z*, or *iz*.

Read each word. Write *s*, *z*, or *iz* to indicate the final *s* sound.

1. pages _____

2. laughs _____

3. hugs _____

4. mixes _____

5. hotels _____

6. eggs _____

7. sings _____

8. boxes _____

9. talks _____

10. calls _____

11. laughs _____

12. learns _____

13. cats _____

14. tries _____

 Home-School Connection Think of five more words with the final /s/ sound. Practice saying the words correctly with a family member.

Comprehension: Biomes All Over the World

Use with Student Book pages 204–209.

Answer the questions about the reading.

Recall

1. How many different kinds of biomes are there on Earth?

_____

2. Which kind of forests have more plant life than any other biome?

_____

3. Why is it hard for plants or animals to live in desert biomes?

_____

_____

Comprehend

4. How are grasslands similar to rain forests? How are they different?

_____

_____

Analyze

5. How do plants and animals adapt to different biomes?

_____

_____

_____

Name _____ Date _____

Reader's Companion

Use with Student Book pages 204–211.

Biomes All Over the World

The arctic tundra is the coldest biome on Earth. Trees do not grow in the tundra. Winds are very strong. Ice covers the ground, and water freezes. Animals such as polar bears must be able to live in the cold. Most animals that live in the tundra have extra fat to keep them warm. Many birds and other animals migrate to a warmer climate for the winter.

In the summer, the weather is warm enough in the tundra for things to grow. Plants and flowers appear. These plants and flowers can live in colder temperatures. Animals that eat plants and grass can find more food during the summer.

Use What You Know

List three animals that might live in the tundra.

1. _____

2. _____

3. _____

Comprehension Check

MARK the TEXT

Underline the parts of the passage that tell you how animals live in the tundra.

Reading Strategy

MARK the TEXT

Describe an animal that might live in the tundra. Circle words in the passage that helped you visualize the animal.

_____

_____

_____

Use the Strategy

How did visualizing help you understand the passage?

_____

_____

_____

Summarize It!

Summarize the passage.

_____

_____

_____

_____

Reader's Response

Would you want to visit the tundra? Why or why not?

_____

_____

_____

Summarize the passage for a family member.

Name _____ Date _____

Learning Strategies: Visualize

Use with Student Book pages 212–213.

Read each passage. Write the words and phrases that helped you form a mental picture of the passage.

The Tundra

1. It is winter in the tundra. An arctic hare sits in the snow. The strong, cold wind blows all around it. The artic hare's white fur coat and a layer of fat keep it warm. The hare's large feet help it stay on top of the snow. Suddenly, the hare is on the move. It darts below the snow, into its den.

_____

_____

Trees in the Rain Forest

2. The Amazon River winds through parts of South America. Most of the land around the river is tropical rain forest. Trees in this rain forest grow as tall as 200 feet! These huge trees need a lot of good soil to grow. Everything a tree needs to grow strong and tall is in the top layer of soil on the forest floor. Roots grow above or near the surface. The roots of rain forest trees spread out from the trunk.

_____

_____

 **Have a family member read or tell you a story. (The family member can use his or her own language.) Write what you visualize from the story and share it with the class.**

Grammar: Comparatives and Superlatives

Use with Student Book pages 214–215.

Review some common **comparatives and superlatives.**

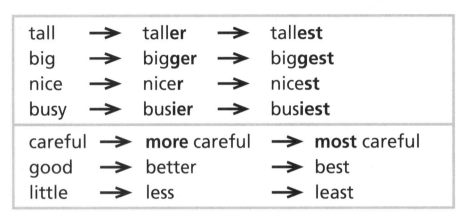

tall	→	tall**er**	→	tall**est**
big	→	big**ger**	→	big**gest**
nice	→	nice**r**	→	nice**st**
busy	→	bus**ier**	→	bus**iest**

careful	→	**more** careful	→	**most** careful
good	→	better	→	best
little	→	less	→	least

Complete the sentences with the correct form of the adjective in parentheses. Add any other necessary words or phrases.

Example: (nice) That painting is <u>nicer than</u> this one.

1. (large) An elephant is _____ a horse.

2. (interesting) I think biology class is _____ than chemistry class.

3. (good) She is the _____ basketball player in our school.

4. (little) There is _____ water in this tank than there is in that one.

5. (cool) Yesterday was the _____ day so far this year.

6. (busy), (careful) That street is _____ now than before and you need to be _____ when you try to cross.

7. (tall) The Willis Tower in Chicago is one of the _____ buildings in the United States right now.

Home-School Connection Write five sentences using comparatives and superlatives. Share your ideas with a family member.

Name _____   Date _____

Spelling: Consonant Clusters *ch* and *tch*

Use with Student Book pages 216–217.

Read each clue. Write the word that matches the clue.

beach	bench
match	peach
pitch	sandwich
scratch	

SPELLING TIP

When a one-syllable word ends with a short vowel and the /ch/ sound, that sound is spelled *ch* or *tch*. Check a dictionary to get the correct spelling.

1. a small cut _____

2. two of a kind _____

3. you sit on it at the park _____

4. you eat this at lunch _____

5. a pretty color or a type of fruit _____

6. a fun place to be in the summer _____

7. to throw a baseball _____

 Write a journal entry using at least four of the words in the box.

_____

_____

_____

 **Home-School Connection** Use a dictionary to find the definitions of three of the words. Show your definitions to a family member.

Writing: Compare and Contrast

Read the paragraph. Then read each question and circle the correct answer.

(1) A temperate rain forest and a tropical rain forest are alike in some ways. (2) Two types of these forests contain many trees and plants. (3) Both also contain many different kinds of mammals and reptiles.

(4) However, there are key differences between the two forests. (5) Temperate forests grow where there are four seasons. (6) Most trees in temperate forests lose their leaves in autumn, when temperatures become cooler.

(7) A rain forest, on the other hand, is hot all year long. (8) It also gets more rain than a temperate forest. (9) This allows trees and bushes to grow all year. (10) Also, the rain forest has a greater variety of plant and animals. (11) More than half of all animals and plants on earth make their home in the rain forest.

1. What is the BEST way to revise sentence 5?

   A Two of these types of forests contain many trees and plants.

   B Both of these forests types contain many trees and plants.

   C Both types of forests contain many trees and plants.

   D No revision is needed.

2. Which sentence could BEST be added after sentence 6?

   A They grow new leaves in the spring.

   B After the autumn is winter.

   C The leaves never grow back.

   D The average temperature in autumn is 68°F.

3. What change, if any, should be made in sentence 8?

   A Change *more* to *more of*

   B Add a comma after *rain*

   C Change *It* to *They*

   D Make no change

Name _____ Date _____

Key Words

Use with Student Book pages 218–219.

organisms
mammals
consumers
producer
predator
scavengers
decomposers

A. Choose the word that *best* completes each sentence. Write the word.

1. The lion is labeled a _____ because it hunts other animals for food.

2. Humans, elephants, and even whales are all types of _____.

3. A creature that makes its own food is a _____.

4. Animals, insects, and even plants are all examples of living _____.

5. A _____ usually eats things that another animal left.

6. Animals that don't make their own food are called _____.

7. Things that help materials break down are _____.

B. Underline the *key word* in each row of letters. Then write a sentence for each word.

8. sdkyscavengerjwxpyql _____

9. wgautconsumerpylbrwom _____

10. mokmammalskrdkuwplbx _____

11. ogwimnlqorganismsujf _____

12. ptpredatorbywczowlmh _____

Academic Words

Use with Student Book page 220.

A. Choose the word that *best* completes each sentence. Write the word.

1. Orange juice is a good _____ of vitamin C.

2. His _____ reason for going to the gym was to become healthier.

3. Milk plays a very important _____ in forming healthy bones and teeth.

B. Choose the word that best matches the meaning of the underlined words. Write the word.

4. A teacher has a very important <u>function</u> in today's society.

   _____

5. Latin was the <u>origin</u> of many of the world's languages.

   _____

6. The <u>most basic</u> goal for many people is to be happy.

   _____

C. Answer the questions.

7. What is your **primary** motive for studying English?

   _____

8. What do you think is the best **source** of information available to us today?

   _____

 Use each academic word in a sentence. Share your sentences with a family member.

Name _____ Date _____

Phonics: Consonant Clusters

Use with Student Book page 221.

> When *r*, *l*, or *s* come together with another consonant at the beginning of a word, the sounds of both letters usually blend together.

bluefish	breathing	close	freshwater
glide	~~place~~	~~predator~~	~~small~~
snap	spout	swim	trouble

A. Write each word from the box in the correct column.

r- blends	*s*- blends	*l*- blends
predator	small	place

B. Read each clue. Write a consonant cluster that completes each word.

1. the color of grass ___ ___ e e n

2. animal with a soft body and an outer shell ___ ___ a i l

3. round, puffy shapes in the sky ___ ___ o u d s

4. a big, black bird ___ ___ o w

Add two more words to each column of the chart. Share your words with a family member.

Comprehension: Marine Food Web

Use with Student Book pages 222–225.

Answer the questions about the reading.

Recall

1. What is the difference between a food chain and a food web?

_____

2. What are two types of plankton?

_____

3. What are some examples of zooplankton? What do they eat?

_____

Comprehend

4. Why are animals like polar bears and orcas at the top of the marine food web?

_____

_____

Analyze

5. How important is the sun to a marine food web?

_____

_____

_____

Name _____ Date _____

Reader's Companion

Use with Student Book pages 222–227.

Marine Food Web

What is the difference between a food chain and food web? A food chain shows one way that energy travels between producers, consumers, and decomposers. A food web shows many food chains that are connected to one another.

Food webs are very important to humans. Any change to one organism in a food web affects all the other organisms in the food web. Natural events, such as hurricanes and earthquakes, cause some major changes to food webs. Humans cause changes to marine food webs by overfishing or pollution. It is important to learn about food webs so that you can help to keep them balanced.

Use What You Know

Make a list of different members of the marine food web.

1. _____

2. _____

3. _____

Comprehension Check

What is a food web? Underline the parts of the passage where you found your answer.

MARK the TEXT

Reading Strategy

What are two important things you learned in the passage? Circle the parts of the passage where you learned this.

_____

_____

Use the Strategy

How did asking questions help you understand the passage?

_____

_____

_____

Summarize It!

Summarize the passage as if you are a teacher explaining what food webs are.

_____

_____

_____

_____

Reader's Response

What can humans do to help take care of food webs?

_____

_____

_____

Summarize the passage for a family member.

Name _____ Date _____

Learning Strategies: Sequence

Use with Student Book pages 228–229.

Read the passage. Answer the question.

Here Comes the Hurricane

The newscaster said a hurricane would hit our area in a few days. First, Mom and my sister went to the store to buy extra food, water, batteries, and other items. Next, Dad and I put the supplies Mom and my sister bought in a waterproof container. Later, Dad and the neighbors helped each other board up windows. Finally, the hurricane came. Mom, Dad, my sister, our dog, and I went to the safest place in the house. We listened to the radio until the newscaster said the hurricane had passed. After the hurricane was over, we went outside to assess the damage.

1. Write the sequence words you find in the passage.

_____

_____

_____

2. Can you think of something else the family should have done? Where do you think it could go in the sequence?

_____

_____

_____

Copyright © by Pearson Education, Inc.

 **Write a sequence of events to describe a chore you do at home. Share your work with a family member.**

133

Grammar: Indefinite Pronouns

Use with Student Book pages 230–231.

Review the list of some common **indefinite pronouns**.

anyone	anybody	anything	(a) few
everyone	everybody	everything	both
someone	somebody	something	many
no one	nobody	nothing	several

Complete the sentences with an appropriate indefinite pronoun. More than one answer may be possible.

Example: <u>Everybody</u> at the party wanted to eat ice cream.

1. _____ told me that there is a test today.

2. He asked _____ for directions to the museum.

3. _____ people saw the car drive away from the store.

4. He was so hungry, he ate _____ on his plate.

5. _____ came to the meeting last week.

6. There was _____ he could do to help the victims of the fire.

7. _____ is possible if you work hard.

8. Carol and Maria are _____ looking for a new backpack.

9. I don't think _____ is ready to take that challenge.

10. _____ animals migrate to warmer climates each year.

 Write five sentences using indefinite pronouns about events you have seen this week. Share your ideas with a family member.

Name _____ Date _____

Spelling: Homophones

Use with Student Book pages 232–233.

Complete each sentence with the correct homophone.

1. ate   eight

My brother is _____ years old.

He _____ everything on his plate.

2. one   won

She had trouble spelling _____ of the words.

I _____ the spelling bee!

3. to   two   too

Kai needs a map _____ the beach.

I want to go, _____.

He is taking his _____ cousins.

✎ **Write a journal entry. Underline the words that are homophones.**

_____

_____

_____

Write definitions for two homophone pairs. Share your definitions with a family member.

Writing: Explain a Process

Read the paragraph. Then read each question and circle the correct answer.

(1) Every seed has a tiny new plant inside of it. (2) How does it grow? (3) First, rain or wind pushes the seed into the earth. (4) Next, the first root grows out from the seed. (5) The root it pushes deep into the soil. (6) Tiny hairs from the root begin to take in water from the ground. (7) Finally, after the root has grown long enough, the plant pokes its head above ground. (8) There has food inside the seed to keep the young plant growing. (9) When the plant forms leaves it is able to make its own food using light from the sun.

1. Which sentence could BEST be added after sentence 3?
   A Sometimes you have to wait for rain.
   B You should plant seeds on windy days.
   C If you don't water plants, they die.
   D Then the seed takes in water.

2. What is the BEST way to revise sentence 5?
   A The root pushes deep into the soil.
   B The root it pushes deep into a soil.
   C Root pushes deep into the soil.
   D No revision is needed.

3. What change, if any, should be made in sentence 8?
   A Change *has* to *its*
   B Change *has* to *are*
   C Change *has* to *is*
   D Make no change

4. What change, if any, should be made in sentence 9?
   A Add a comma after *able*
   B Add a comma after *forms*
   C Add a comma after *leaves*
   D Make no change.

Name _____ Date _____

Key Words

Use with Student Book pages 234–235.

| endangered |
| litter |
| pollution |
| illegal |
| conservation |
| protect |

A. **Choose the word that *best* completes each sentence. Write the word.**

1. I always feel very angry when I see people
_____ by throwing paper
on the street.

2. The giant panda is one of the world's most famous
_____ animals.

3. Volunteers all over the world work very hard to
_____ the environment.

4. _____ is one of the major concerns for people
living in big cities.

5. It is _____ in most places to throw trash on
the street.

6. _____ is one way to save natural resources.

B. **Choose the word that best matches the meaning of the underlined words. Write the word.**

7. I never see people <u>throw trash</u> on the floor in our classroom.
_____

8. Zookeepers work very hard to <u>take care of</u> endangered animals.
_____

9. It is <u>against the law</u> to drive without a license.
_____

10. The air was so full of <u>dirt and smoke</u>, I could hardly breathe.
_____

137

Academic Words

Use with Student Book page 236.

contribute
cycle
enabled

A. Choose the word that *best* completes each sentence. Write the word.

1. Airplanes _____ people to travel over long distances quickly.

2. I always try to _____ to at least one charity each year.

3. One year equals one _____ of the seasons.

B. Match each word with its definition. Write the letter of the correct answer.

4. contribute _____

5. cycle _____

6. enabled _____

A made something possible

B something that repeats itself

C to give or supply something

C. Answer the questions.

7. What is something people might **contribute** to?

_____

8. What things can you think of that happen in a **cycle**?

_____

9. What is one thing that **enabled** people to live more comfortably?

_____

Home-School Connection Use each academic word in a sentence. Share your sentences with a family member.

Name _____ Date _____

Word Study: Commonly Confused Words

Use with Student Book page 237.

> Words that sound the same, or almost the same, but have different spellings and meanings can cause problems for writers.

Read each clue. Circle the correct word for each sentence. Then write the word.

1. Clue: Which word means *a single thing*?

_____ river is over there. (Won, One)

2. Clue: Which word means *caused to go*?

A boat was _____ to rescue us. (sent, cent)

3. Clue: Which word means *listened with your ears*?

We _____ the boat horn honking. (herd, heard)

4. Clue: Which word means *belonging to us*?

The rescuers asked us _____ names. (our, hour)

5. Clue: Which word means *body around which Earth revolves*?

The _____ was still out, so we had plenty of light. (sun, son)

6. Clue: Which word means *part of a plant*?

Each _____ was red and yellow. (flour, flower)

Think of another pair of commonly confused words. Use each word in a sentence. Show your sentences to a family member.

Comprehension: Save the Sea Turtles

Use with Student Book pages 238–243.

Answer the questions about the reading.

Recall

1. Where do Kemp's ridley sea turtles make their nests?

_____

2. What does a female turtle do after laying her eggs?

_____

3. Why do fishermen refuse to use the special nets required by the government?

_____

Comprehend

4. What are some ways you can get involved in helping the Kemp's ridley turtles?

_____

_____

Analyze

5. What were some facts you learned in this article on Kemp's ridley turtles?

_____

_____

_____

Name _____ Date _____

Reader's Companion

Use with Student Book pages 238–243.

Save the Sea Turtles

By the 1960s, the United States and Mexico realized that the Kemp's ridley turtles were in terrible danger. These governments passed laws making taking turtle eggs illegal.

Many turtles still died. Many choked on the plastic bags littering the ocean. Many more were trapped in shrimp fishing nets and drowned.

In 1989, the U.S. government passed a law requiring shrimp fishermen to use a special net with openings at the bottom and the top that allows larger animals like turtles and sharks to swim free. This law has helped a little. Gradually, more turtles are coming to Padre Island to nest each year. However, there are still major threats to the safety of Kemp's ridley turtles, especially pollution and litter. In 2010, for example, an oil rig exploded and caused 4.9 million gallons of oil to spill into the Gulf of Mexico. The spilled oil damaged the beaches where Kemp's ridley turtles nest and the water where they live.

Use What You Know

List three reasons why Kemp's ridley turtles became endangered.

1. _____

2. _____

3. _____

Genre

MARK the TEXT

Underline the parts of the passage that gave you information about what laws were passed to help the turtles.

Reading Strategy

Circle the opinion in the passage. How do you know it is not a fact?

Use the Strategy

How did identifying fact and opinion help you understand the passage?

_____

_____

_____

Summarize It!

Summarize the passage.

_____

_____

_____

_____

Reader's Response

Should people help endangered animals? Why or why not?

_____

_____

_____

Home-School Connection Summarize the passage for a family member.

Name _____ Date _____

Learning Strategies: Identify Fact and Opinion

For use with Student Book pages 244–245.

Read the passage and answer the questions.

Where's the Goalie?

I go to a very small school. The school is so small that there are exactly 11 players on our soccer team. José is our goalie. He works very hard to keep the other team from scoring goals. He is the best goalie ever! My team has a very important game today. It is the final game of the season. José is sick. He has a very bad cold. His mother told him to stay in bed today. What can we do?

1. What are the facts in the passage?

_____

_____

2. What are the opinions in the passage?

_____

_____

Home-School Connection Look through a newspaper. What information is fact? What is opinion? Share what you learned with the class.

Grammar: Transitional Words

Use with Student Book pages 246–247.

Review the list of some common **transitional words**.

however	also	in addition	as well as	instead
for example	therefore	as a result	for this reason	

Choose the best transitional word for each sentence. Write the word.

Example: (however / as well as) Everybody wanted to go swimming. <u>However</u>, it was raining.

1. (however / therefore) I want to go to college one day. _____, I study hard everyday.

2. (for example / instead) People contribute to the litter problem. _____, they throw trash on the ground.

3. (instead / for this reason) New technology is making space travel possible. _____, many people may soon be able to travel to space.

4. (however / also) I like sports. _____, I like music, too.

5. (also / such as) He is a member of the debate team. _____, he is president of his class.

6. (instead / for example) That fireman is a courageous person. _____, he risked his life to save a little girl.

7. (therefore / on the other hand) I really want to join the track team. _____, baseball sounds like fun, too.

 Write five sentences using five different transitional words. Share your ideas with a family member.

Name _____   Date _____

Spelling: Adding -ed or -ing to Verbs

Use with Student Book pages 248–249.

Make new words by adding -ed or -ing. The first one is done for you.

1. drop

   add -ed   dropped _____

   add -ing _____

2. watch

   add -ed _____

   add -ing _____

3. grab

   add -ed _____

   add -ing _____

4. work

   add -ed _____

   add -ing _____

> ### SPELLING TIP
> You can simply add -ed or -ing to many one-syllable verbs. However, with one-syllable verbs ending in a stressed CVC or CCVC pattern, you will need to double the final consonant, as in *swimming.*

 Write a short paragraph that uses three words with -ed or -ing endings.

_____
_____
_____

 **Think of five more words that have the -ed/-ing pattern. Write each form of the words. Show your work to a family member.**

Writing: Organize Ideas by Cause and Effect

Read the paragraph. Then read each question and circle the correct answer.

(1) The ocelot is a small wildcat with golden fur and black spots. (2) For this reason, it is sometimes called "America's little leopard." (3) About 200 years ago there were many ocelots living in the grasslands of the southern United States. (4) Today, there are fewer than 100 left. (5) The area is now covered with cattle ranches and farms. (6) Also, ocelots have fewer places to make their homes. (7) Roads and highways are another problem for ocelots. (8) More ocelots die from being hit by cars and trucks than from any other cause. (9) Also, there is hope for America's "little leopard." (10) Many landowners are restoring grasslands to give ocelots a place to live. (11) In addition, the government is building underpasses to help ocelots cross roads safely.

1. What is the BEST way to revise sentence 6?
    A Change *Also* to *As a result*
    B Change *fewer* to *less*
    C Change *places* to *place*
    D No revision is needed.

2. What change, if any, should be made in sentence 9?
    A Change *hope* to *some hope*
    B Change *there is* to *it is*
    C Change *Also* to *However*
    D Make no change

3. Which sentence could BEST be added after sentence 11?
    A I am not sure what will happen to the ocelot.
    B People driving cars should be careful.
    C There are many other endangered animals now.
    D Soon, the ocelot may no longer be endangered.

Name _____ Date _____

Review

Use with Student Book pages 194–249.

Answer the questions after reading Unit 4. You can go back and reread to help find the answers.

1. Refer to *Biomes All Over the World*. Compare and contrast how mountains and tundras are similar and different.

How Mountains and Tundras Are Similar	How Mountains and Tundras Are Different

2. Which words best describe a *tropical* climate? Circle the letter of the correct answer.

A cold and dry   **C** hot and dry
B hot and humid   **D** covered with water

3. Why are oceans important?

_____

_____

_____

4. What is the difference between a food chain and food web?

_____

_____

5. What are some examples of *consumers* and *decomposers*?

_____

_____

6. What do *decomposers* eat? Circle all that are correct.

    A waste products of other organisms

    B predators

    C dead animals and plants

    D lobsters

7. Why is the Kemp's ridley turtle endangered?

_____

_____

8. What is the government doing to help this turtle?

_____

_____

9. What can we do to help endangered species?

_____

_____

Home-School Connection Tell a family member something new you learned in this unit.

Name _____   Date _____

Writing Workshop:
Write a Compare-and-Contrast Essay

Read the passage. Then read each question on the next page and circle the correct answer.

Cat Person or Dog Person?

(1) Are you a cat person or a dog person? (2) Both animal can be great pets. (3) But some people like dogs better, and some like cats better.

(4) If you say "Come!" to a dog, it usually come to you. (5) Cats don't come when you call them. (6) I have both a cat and a dog. (7) Cats only come to you when they want to.

(8) Dogs can be noisy. (9) Also, cats are usually quiet. (10) My cat likes to sit next to me when I do my homework.

(11) Both animals like attention. (12) Unlike cats, I have to take my dog for a walk every day. (13) Sometimes I feel too tired to go.

(14) What kind of person am I? (15) I like them both. (16) My dog and my cat are my friends.

1. What change, if any, should be made in sentence 2?
   A Change *animal* to *animals*
   B Change *be* to *are*
   C Change *pets* to *pet*
   D Make no change

2. What change, if any, should be made in sentence 4?
   A Change *say* to *says*
   B Change *come* to *comes*
   C Change *!* to *?*
   D Make no change

3. What is the BEST way to revise sentence 9?
   A Also, cats are more usually quiet.
   B However, cats are usually quiet.
   C Therefore, cats are usually quiet.
   D No revision is needed.

4. What change, if any, should be made in sentence 13?
   A Change *too* to *to*
   B Change *to go* to *going*
   C Change *tired* to *tried*
   D Make no change

5. Which sentence does NOT belong in this essay?
   A Sentence 2
   B Sentence 6
   C Sentence 8
   D Sentence 12

Name _____ Date _____

Fluency

Use with Student Book page 257.

How fast are you? Use a clock. Read the text about *Marine Food Web*. How long did it take you? Write your time in the chart. Read three times.

Marine Food Web describes how humans, animals, and plants	9
affect each other in different ways in food webs. Food webs are very	22
important to humans. Changes to one organism in a food	32
web affects other organisms. Natural events such as hurricanes and	42
earthquakes can cause changes. Humans cause changes too, through	51
overfishing and pollution. It is important to keep food webs in	62
balance.	63
The marine food web starts with the sun, which gives energy to	74
tiny plants that live in the water. Tiny animals move through the	86
water and eat the tiny plants. Small fish eat the plankton, and then	99
larger fish and mammals feed on the smaller fish. Other animals that	111
do not spend their entire lives in the water, such as penguins,	123
elephant seals, and polar bears, also eat the fish.	132
We are all producers, consumers, or decomposers in food webs.	142

My Times

Learning Checklist

Check off what you have learned well. Review as needed.

Word Study and Phonics

☐ Final *s* sound (*z*, *s*, *iz*)

☐ Consonant Clusters

☐ Commonly Confused Words

Strategies

☐ Visualize

☐ Ask Questions

☐ Sequence

☐ Identify Fact and Opinion

Grammar

☐ Comparatives and Superlatives

☐ Indefinite Pronouns

☐ Transitional Words

Writing

☐ Compare and Contrast

☐ Explain a Process

☐ Organize Ideas by Cause and Effect

☐ Writing Workshop: Write a Compare-and-Contrast Essay

Listening and Speaking

☐ Listening and Speaking Workshop: Give a How-to Presentation

Name _____ Date _____

Test Preparation

Use with Student Book pages 258–259.

Read the selection and the chart. Then answer the questions.

1	2	3	4	5
Female sea turtle arrives on the beach.	_____ _____ _____	Female sea turtle returns to the sea.	Young sea turtles (called hatchlings) hatch.	Hatchlings go into the sea where they live and grow.

1   When the female turtle is ready to lay her eggs, she comes out of the water and onto the beach. There, she digs a nest. The nest looks like a hole in the sand. She lays her eggs in the hole and covers them up with sand. Hiding the eggs makes it hard for predators to find the eggs and eat them.

2   The hatchlings, or baby turtles, are in great danger as soon as they hatch. Many animals and birds think the hatchlings are a tasty meal. The hatchlings run as fast as they can into the sea. With luck, they will grow up and have their own young.

1. What is the first thing the female turtle does when she is ready to lay her eggs?
   A She covers up the nest of eggs.
   B She lays her eggs in the water.
   C She arrives on the beach.
   D She digs a hole in the sand.

2. Why do the baby turtles run into the sea after they hatch?
   F Many birds and animals like to eat them.
   G It is too hot for them to live on the beach.

   H The male sea turtle wants to eat the hatchlings.
   J The hatchlings are not in danger on the beach.

3. Look at the chart. Which of these belongs on the blank line?
   F Female sea turtle swims and lays her eggs in the water.
   G Female sea turtle digs a hole in the sand and lays eggs.
   H The hatchlings dig holes.
   J The hatchings grow up.

Read the selection and the chart. Then answer the questions.

1	2	3	4	5
The author starts running in Ecuador.	_____ _____ _____	The author moves to the U.S.	The author joins school track and field team.	Someday the author will run a marathon.

I started running when I lived in Ecuador. I rode the bus to school each day, one hour each way. Then I sat in school all day. I knew I needed some exercise.

At first, I only had an old pair of running shoes, but they were enough to start! Then I bought some better running shoes, and I started running for one hour each day. Running made me feel great!

Soon after that, I moved to the United States. I saw that running is very popular here. I joined my school's track and field team. Now I run 20 miles every week. Someday I want to run a marathon. That's more than 26 miles. I can't wait!

1. The main character started running because she—
   A lived in Ecuador
   B got new running shoes
   C needed to get more exercise
   D joined the track and field team

2. What is the paragraph mostly about?
   F Track and field
   G A marathon
   H Moving to the United States
   J Becoming a runner

3. Look at the chart. Which of these belongs on the blank line?
   F The author feels great.
   G The author has an old pair of running shoes.
   H The author rides the school bus.
   J The author gets new running shoes.

Name _____ Date _____

Key Words
Use with Student Book pages 266–267.

instruments
percussion
vibrations
notes
composition
award

A. Choose the word that *best* fits each definition. Write the word.

1. objects used for making musical sounds

_____

2. a piece of work, something you write _____

3. the individual sounds in a musical piece _____

4. something you win for doing something well _____

5. continuous shaking movements _____

6. instruments that make sounds when they are hit

_____

B. Choose the word that *best* completes each sentence. Write the word.

7. Drums and cymbals are different _____ instruments.

8. I can play many different _____, but Eva can only play the saxophone.

9. Some singers can sing higher _____ than others.

10. You can both hear and feel _____.

11. This musical group has won an _____ for its performances.

Academic Words

Use with Student Book page 268.

achievements
cease
perceive

A. Choose the word that *best* completes each sentence. Write the word.

1. The construction went on for months and did not _____ .

2. His paintings are his greatest_____ .

3. I could _____ an animal moving through the bushes.

B. Choose the word that best matches the underlined words. Write the word.

4. He did not <u>recognize</u> the source of the light.

_____

5. The rain did not <u>end</u> for many days and caused large floods.

_____

6. His many <u>accomplishments</u> in science were recognized around the world.

_____

C. Answer the questions.

7. What is one of your greatest **achievements**?

_____

8. What is something that does not **cease**?

_____

 Use each academic word in a sentence. Share your sentences with a family member.

Name _____ Date _____

Phonics: Past -*ed* ending *id, d, t*
Use with Student Book page 269.

> The -*ed* ending can be pronounced as *d* , *t* , or as *id*, a separate syllable.

Write each verb in the correct column of the chart. The first one is done for you.

~~added~~	constructed	flapped	grated
greeted	opened	started	stayed
stopped	traded	watered	worked

-*ed* adds a syllable	-*ed* does not add a syllable
added	_____
_____	_____
_____	_____
_____	_____
_____	_____
_____	_____

Home-School Connection Find verbs with the -*ed* ending in a magazine or newspaper. Read aloud your examples to a family member.

Comprehension:
Touching Sound with Evelyn Glennie

Use with Student Book pages 270–273.

Answer the questions about the reading.

Recall

1. Where did Evelyn Glennie grow up?

_____

2. Before percussion, what instrument did Evelyn play as a child?

_____

3. What does "perfect pitch" mean?

_____

Comprehend

4. What does Evelyn do when she is not performing music?

_____

_____

Analyze

5. How can someone become a great musician like Evelyn?

_____

_____

_____

Name _____ Date _____

Reader's Companion

Use with Student Book pages 270–273.

Touching Sound with Evelyn Glennie

Evelyn grew up on a farm in Scotland. There was a piano in her home. As a young child, she asked her parents to let her take piano lessons. They let her take lessons when she was eight years old. Evelyn soon found out she had what musicians call "perfect pitch." She could hear the notes perfectly in her mind. This was good, because she was slowly losing her hearing.

Evelyn found that hearing aids kept her from being able to perceive sounds with the rest of her body. She stopped wearing them when she was 12 years old. Evelyn knew she could hear the correct music notes in her mind. She also used her body to feel the vibrations the instruments made. She learned to play many percussion instruments. This surprised her teachers, who thought Evelyn would not be able to play music once she lost her hearing.

Use What You Know

List three things you know about people that cannot hear.

1. _____

2. _____

3. _____

Comprehension Check

Draw a circle around three details in the passage.

Reading Strategy

What is the main idea of this passage? Underline where you found the answer.

Use the Strategy

How did identifying the main idea and details help you understand the passage?

_____

_____

_____

Summarize It!

Summarize the passage.

_____

_____

_____

_____

Reader's Response

Which percussion instrument(s) do you like best? Why?

_____

_____

_____

Home-School Connection

Summarize the passage for a family member.

Name _____ Date _____

Learning Strategies: Main Idea and
Details

Use with Student Book pages 274–275.

Read the passage. Write the main idea and three details.

The Percussion Section

Mrs. Jones, the music teacher, put an announcement on the school bulletin board. She was holding auditions for the orchestra. My friends and I were so excited. We asked Mrs. Jones what kinds of players she was looking for. She said she really needed people to play percussion instruments. She said it was hard to get people to play percussion instruments because the players had to stand at the back of the orchestra to play. Also, the instruments were very loud, so parents didn't want their kids to practice them at home. My friends and I said we would be happy to play the percussion instruments. Ronnie told Mrs. Jones we could practice after school. He auditioned to play the snare drum. I auditioned to play the bass drum. Juanita auditioned to play the triangles, cymbals, and rattles. Mrs. Jones was very happy. "Now we can have a full orchestra," she said.

Main Idea: _____

Detail: _____

Detail: _____

Detail: _____

Have a family member read or tell you a story. (The family member can use his or her own language.) Tell your family member the main idea and three details from the story.

Grammar: Subordinating Conjunctions

Use with Student Book pages 276–277.

Review the list of these common **subordinating conjuctions**.

after	although	as	because	before	if
once	since	though	until	when	while

Complete the sentences with one of the subordinate conjunctions from the list above. More than one answer may be possible.

Example: <u>Although</u> he is very talented, Jacob is lazy.

1. _____ buying a new computer, compare prices.

2. _____ I was riding my bicycle, I saw many people walking their dogs.

3. _____ he worked hard, he became a success at an early age.

4. _____ you want to conserve energy, you should turn off the lights.

5. _____ he was a pioneer in his field, people often asked him for advice.

6. _____ you agree to a challenge, you need to focus on the results.

7. _____ you want to contribute something to society, you should become a volunteer.

8. _____ I identified the problem, I couldn't fix it.

9. _____ the doorbell rang, the dog began to bark.

 Write five sentences about your day using subordinating conjunctions. Share your ideas with a family member.

Name _____ Date _____

Spelling: Finding Related Words

Use with Student Book pages 278–279.

Read each word. Write the smaller word found in it.

1. performance _____

2. climber _____

3. selection _____

4. mixture _____

5. graphic _____

6. soloist _____

7. oily _____

8. throughout _____

9. musical _____

10. wonderful _____

SPELLING TIP

Thinking of a related word will help you spell a word you don't know. For example, remembering *crumble* can help you spell *crumb* correctly.

Write a journal entry using at least four of the words above.

_____

_____

_____

 **Find five words that contain a related word in a newspaper or magazine. Show your words to a family member.**

163

Writing: Problem and Solution

Read the paragraph. Then read each question and circle the correct answer.

(1) Sand is washing away on many beaches. (2) After years of crashing waves and wind some beaches are in danger of disappearing. (3) What can be done to save these beaches?

4) One idea is to place large tree branch on the sand in winter to keep it from blowing or washing away. (5) However, the branches might be washed out to sea when there are strong winds and storms.

(6) Another, maybe better, solution is to plant trees or bushes along the beach. (7) The roots would hold the sand in place, and the branches would help stop it from blowing away. (8) People at the beach would enjoy the trees. (9) People could do research to find trees that like sandy soil. (10) Then they could raise money to buy the trees. (11) Finally, they could plant the trees and see how that works.

1. What is the BEST way to revise sentence 2?

   A Add a comma after *wind*

   B Add a comma after *waves*

   C Add a comma after *beaches*

   D No revision is needed.

2. What change, if any, should be made in sentence 4?

   A Change *it* to *them*

   B Change *branch* to *branches*

   C Change *One* to *The*

   D Make no change

3. Which sentence does NOT belong in this paragraph?

   A Sentence 3

   B Sentence 5

   C Sentence 8

   D Sentence 9

Name _____ Date _____

Key Words

Use with Student Book pages 280–281.

| code |
| escape |
| landmarks |
| border |
| riverbank |
| tracks |

A. Choose the word that *best* completes each sentence. Write the word.

1. The statues in town are _____.

2. When you get away from something, you

_____.

3. The land next to a river is a _____.

4. Your footprints in the sand can also be called

_____.

5. The river served as a _____ between the two states.

6. A _____ is a group of words, phrases, or symbols that has a special meaning.

B. Read the pairs of sentences. One makes sense. The other is silly. Write an S next to each sentence that makes sense. Write an X next to each silly sentence.

7. A river has two <u>riverbanks</u>. _____

A river has ten <u>riverbanks</u>. _____

8. You can find the horse by following its <u>tracks</u>. _____

You can lose the horse by following its <u>tracks</u>. _____

Academic Words

Use with Student Book page 282.

> instruct
> **specific**
> symbols

A. Choose the word that *best* completes each sentence. Write the word.

1. The coach addressed a _____ problem our team was having.

2. The alphabet is an important series of _____ we use to write.

3. It is important for a doctor to _____ people about a healthy diet.

B. Match each word with its definition. Write the letter of the correct answer.

4. instruct _____   **A** special, precise, or particular

5. specific _____   **B** something that represents another thing

6. symbols _____   **C** to give orders or knowledge

C. Answer the questions.

7. What are some **symbols** you see around you everyday?

_____

8. Who is someone you know that **instructs** other people?

_____

 **Use each academic word in a sentence. Share your sentences with a family member.**

Name _____ Date _____

Word Study: Figurative Language

Use with Student Book page 283.

> Writers sometimes use **figurative language** to paint word pictures.

Read each sentence. Underline the figurative language in each sentence. Then write what you think it means.

1. The volcano <u>coughed rock and ash</u>.

The volcano erupted. _____

2. Her smile lit up my heart.

_____

3. The breeze whispered through the leaves.

_____

4. I ate so much that I'm going to explode.

_____

5. All the trees bowed with respect to the wind.

_____

6. His mouth runs like a motor.

_____

7. Her eyes sparkled like stars.

_____

8. Xiao can run like the wind.

_____

Comprehension: A Song Map

Use with Student Book pages 284–287.

Answer the questions about the reading.

Recall

1. What does the Big Dipper look like? How is it significant in the song?

_____

2. How did Peg Leg Joe get his name?

_____

3. What is the landmark where the river ends betweens two hills?

_____

Comprehend

4. How did Peg Leg Joe help the slaves escape to freedom?

_____

_____

Analyze

5. How do you think slaves learned *Follow the Drinking Gourd* and its code?

_____

_____

_____

Name _____ Date _____

Reader's Companion

Use with Student Book pages 284–287.

A Song Map

Who was the old man waiting to carry them to freedom? Some people believe he was Peg Leg Joe, a former sailor who helped slaves. Peg Leg Joe used a wooden leg.

Chorus
Follow the drinking gourd!
Follow the drinking gourd!
For the old man is waiting for to carry you to freedom
If you follow the drinking gourd.

Stanza 2
The riverbank makes a very good road,
The dead trees will show you the way,
Left foot, peg foot traveling on,
Following the drinking gourd.

Some people say Peg Leg Joe marked trees and other landmarks along the riverbank. This helped the slaves make sure they were going in the right direction. These tracks, or marks, were often a mud or charcoal outline of a human left foot and another mark. Some people believe the other mark was Peg Leg Joe's wooden leg.

Use What You Know

List three ways to create a secret code.

1. _____

2. _____

3. _____

Comprehension Check

Underline the directions given in Stanza 2.

Genre

What marks did Peg Leg Joe leave? Circle the text where you find the answer.

169

Use the Strategy

How did summarizing help you understand the passage?

_____

_____

_____

Summarize It!

Summarize the directions the song gave slaves.

_____

_____

_____

_____

Reader's Response

What other kinds of messages can you find in songs?

_____

_____

_____

Home-School Connection   **Summarize the passage for a family member.**

Name _____ Date _____

Learning Strategies: Make Inferences

Use with Student Book pages 288–289.

Read the passage. Answer the questions.

Landmarks

Have you ever seen a landmark? You probably have. Landmarks are everywhere! People like to visit these important places. Some landmarks honor important people from the past. Are there any statues in your town? Statues can be landmarks. Many landmarks tell about the history of a place. The Statue of Liberty is an important landmark. It tells about the history of New York and the United States. The Gateway Arch in Missouri and The Alamo in Texas are two other important American landmarks. What landmarks do you have in your town?

1. What is this passage about?

_____

2. What do landmarks represent?

_____

3. Why do people like to visit landmarks?

_____

4. How does something become a landmark?

_____

Copyright © by Pearson Education, Inc.

Listen to a song with a family member. The song can be in your own language. Discuss an inference you can make from the song with the family member.

171

Grammar: Prepositions and Prepositional Phrases

Use with Student Book pages 290–291.

Review the list of some common **prepositions.**

on	at	in	between	from	under
in front of	inside	next to	until	by	to
into	along	toward	without	except	above

Complete the sentences with one of prepositions from the list above. More than one answer may be possible.

Example: The plant is <u>next to</u> the bookshelf.

1. The pilot flew the airplane _____ the two mountains.

2. I always stand _____ Chen and Antonio in the lunch line.

3. The cattle were all eating grass _____ the pasture.

4. Everyone came to see my show _____ my grandmother.

5. In an emergency, sometimes people have to leave their homes _____ their things.

6. At the park, a bird flew right _____ my head.

7. There are beautiful grasslands _____ the border of that country.

8. He hid the money _____ the bed so no one would find it.

9. There are some important symbols _____ that painting.

10. The mechanic put his wrench _____ the top of the engine.

 **Home-School Connection** Write five sentences using prepositional phrases. Share your ideas with a family member.

Name _____ Date _____

Spelling: /j/ Sound Spelled with *g*

Use with Student Book pages 292–293.

gem	general	generous
genius	geography	giant
ginger	giraffe	

Read each clue. Write the word that matches the clue.

1. an animal with a long neck _____

2. a very smart person _____

3. huge, very big _____

4. a jewel or precious stone _____

5. a spice _____

6. only the main features of something _____

7. willing to give time or money to another _____

8. study of the countries of the world _____

 Write a paragraph using at least four words that have the /j/ sound spelled with *g*. You can choose words from the box above.

_____

_____

_____

 Write the meanings of four words with the /j/ sound spelled with *g*.
Share your work with a family member.

Writing: Write a Response to Literature

Read the paragraph. Then read each question and circle the correct answer.

(1) <u>The Lost Lake</u>, by Allen Say, grabbed my attention and did not let go. (2) It tells the story of Luke and his father. (3) Luke goes to visit his father in the city, but his father is very busy. (4) He does not pay much attention to Luke then one day he takes Luke on a hike. (5) They discover more than just a lost lake. (6) They discover that they like the same things and have a strong relationship.

(7) I think the author has created characters that act as real fathers and sons do. (8) It is a very believable story. (9) It reminded me of going camping with my brother and father last summer—we all got to know each other better.

(10) I learned about how relationships can change after reading this book. (11) In fact, it helped me to understand my father a little better.

1. What is the BEST way to revise sentence 4?

    A Add a comma after *attention*

    B Add a comma after *day*

    C Add a period after the first *Luke*

    D No revision is needed.

2. What change, if any, should be made in sentence 9?

    A Change *each other* to *another*

    B Change *each other* to *each other's*

    C Change *each other* to *other*

    D Make no change

3. Which sentence could BEST be added after sentence 9?

    A That's what happens to Luke and his father.

    B It was just like a story.

    C I like going camping with my family.

    D I can't believe they went camping.

Name _____ Date _____

Key Words

Use with Student Book pages 294–295.

A. Choose the word that best completes each sentence. Write the word.

1. Jake and Kelly sang a lovely _____ for the school talent contest.

2. Her concert _____ last year was a huge success.

3. _____ is a kind of music developed in the United States that was popular with the cowboys.

4. A type of music that is a mix of rock and roll and country music is called _____ .

5. That song brings out strong _____ in some people who hear it.

6. His _____ has lasted more than 40 years.

B. Write TRUE or FALSE.

7. Country and western is a kind of food. _____

8. A professional football player has a career in sports. _____

9. Rockabilly is originally a British style of music. _____

10. *Tour* is another word for traveling. _____

11. Someone who has strong emotions seldom cries. _____

12. A duet is sung by three people. _____

Academic Words

Use with Student Book page 296.

achieved

enormous

status

A. Choose the word that *best* completes each sentence. Write the word.

1. The professor _____ great progress in his research last year.

2. Finding a new type of clean fuel would be an _____ discovery.

3. Her help with the refugees gave her a place of high _____ in the village.

B. Underline the *academic word* in each row of letters. Then write a sentence for each word.

4. bgewkopstatuswqolmhp _____

5. ntxpjukpachievedjnta _____

6. zyekoenormoushtemsrp _____

C. Answer the questions.

7. What animal could you describe as **enormous**?

   _____

8. What is something you have **achieved** in the last year?

   _____

9. Who is someone with **status** in your school?

   _____

 **Use each academic word in a sentence. Share your sentences with a family member.**

Name _____ Date _____

Phonics: Words with *ow, ou*

Use with Student Book page 297.

> The diphthong /*ou*/ can be spelled as either *ou* or *ow*.
> Sometimes *ow* can make a long *o* sound. If one sound
> doesn't make sense, try the other.

Read each clue. Fill in the blank with vowels to complete the word.
Practice saying each word with a partner.

1. move a ball up and down   b _____ nce

2. a lot of people in one place   cr _____ d

3. do this in a boat   r _____

4. opposite of up   d _____ n

5. something you might live in   h _____ se

6. not to lead, but to   foll _____

7. a person, place, or thing   n _____ n

8. a king or queen wears this   cr _____ n

9. a cat likes to chase one   m _____ se

10. covers the ground in winter   sn _____

Home-School Connection Look through a newspaper or magazine. Find six more words that
are spelled with *ou* or *ow*. Show your words to a family member.

177

Comprehension: Elvis Presley/Austin: The Live Music Capital of the World

Use with Student Book pages 298–303.

Answer the questions about the reading.

Recall

1. Who taught Elvis Presley how to play guitar?

_____

2. How much did Elvis pay to record his first two songs?

_____

3. What is Elvis's nickname?

_____

Comprehend

4. How did Austin get its reputation as a music town?

_____

_____

Analyze

5. What other singers do you know who have trademarks like Stevie Ray Vaughan's hat?

_____

_____

_____

Name _____ Date _____

Reader's Companion

Use with Student Book pages 298–303.

Austin: The Live Music Capital of the World

An important event in Austin's music history occurred in 1975. A 30-minute music show was taped at the University of Texas at Austin. Willie Nelson was there. The show presented Texas musicians, many of whom lived in Austin. That show, *Austin City Limits*, is now the longest running music show on television, and is seen in countries around the globe. Thousands of musicians, from the unknown to music legends, have been on the show, playing music from country and western to folk to rock. The *Austin City Limits* scenery is famous. The musicians play against a picture of Austin at night.

Use What You Know

List three famous musicians who come from Texas.

1. _____

2. _____

3. _____

Comprehension Check

Where is *Austin City Limits* shown on TV? Underline the parts of the passage where you found your answers.

MARK the TEXT

Genre

MARK the TEXT

Circle the part of the passage that explains where *Austin City Limits* is recorded.

Use the Strategy

Why is it helpful to identify the author's purpose as you read?

_____

_____

_____

Summarize It!

Summarize the passage.

_____

_____

_____

_____

Reader's Response

Who is your favorite musician? Why?

_____

_____

_____

Summarize the passage for a family member.

Name _____ Date _____

Learning Strategies: Author's Purpose

Use with Student Book pages 304–305.

Read the passage. Answer the questions.

Join the Eagletown Marching Band

Have you ever wanted to make music? Would you like to march in parades? Do you dream of performing in a large stadium? This is your big chance! Don't worry! You don't have to be a great musician. We will even teach you how to play an instrument. The Eagletown Marching Band needs drum players and horn players. We even need a few people to play the kazoo! What do you have to do? Just come to the tryouts this Saturday at the high school. We'll be there from noon until five o'clock. If you want to meet new people and have a great time, come and join the Eagletown Marching Band!

1. What is the author's purpose?

_____

_____

2. Explain how you found your answer.

_____

_____

3. How did identifying the author's purpose help you understand the text?

_____

_____

Read a newspaper or magazine article with a family member. Tell a family member about the author's purpose.

Grammar: Present Perfect

Use with Student Book pages 306–307.

Review how to form the **present perfect tense**.

> I **have studied** French for five years.
> She **has played** the piano since she was young.
> They **haven't finished** writing the report yet.

Complete the sentences with the present perfect form of the verb in parenthesis.

Example: (see) I <u>have seen</u> a horror movie before.

1. (grow) You _____ since the last time I saw you.

2. (achieve) He _____ many things in his long career.

3. (think) I _____ about you many times today.

4. (feel) She _____ sick for the past few days.

5. (not finish) They _____ their projects yet.

6. (be) We _____ to a rockabilly concert before.

7. (like) William _____ Anita for a very long time.

8. (not be) He _____ to see the dentist in over a year.

9. (instruct) The coach _____ us to wear a uniform tomorrow.

10. (fly) The pilot _____ more than one-hundred solo flights.

 **Write five sentences using the present perfect tense. Share your ideas with a family member.**

Name _____ Date _____

Spelling: Words with Silent Letters

Use with Student Book pages 308–309.

SPELLING TIP

Learn to spell words with silent letters and hard spellings by saying them aloud exactly as they are spelled.

Say each word including the silent letter. Then use each word in a sentence. The first one is done for you.

1. wrist   wuh-rist   <u>My sister broke her wrist.</u>

2. knee   kuh-nee   _____

3. handsome   hand-sum   _____

4. ghost   guh-host   _____

5. often   off-ten   _____

6. island   i-sland   _____

7. toward   to-ward   _____

8. soften   sof-ten   _____

 Write a journal entry using at least three words with silent letters. Show your work to a partner.

_____

_____

_____

 **Make a list of five more words with silent letters. Show your list to a family member.**

Writing: Write an Article About a Musician

Read the article. Then read each question and circle the correct answer.

(1) Miley Cyrus is only 18 years old, but she has already had more success than people twice her age. (2) She is one of the most exciting pop singers in the world. (3) Cyrus is the daughter of the country singer Billy Ray Cyrus. (4) Her road to fame began in 2006 when she won the title role in the Hannah Montana TV series.

(5) Once the TV show was a success, Cyrus made her own album. (6) Meet Miley Cyrus was released in 2007 it was a big success. (7) The single from the album was called "See You Again." (8) It made the Top 10. (9) The album went to #1 on the charts.

(10) In 2008, Cyrus made another album. (11) It was called Breakout. (12) Miley Cyrus definitely has a bright future ahead of her.

1. What change, if any, should be made in sentence 1?

   A Change *success* to *successful*

   B Change *age* to *ages*

   C Change *is* to *has*

   D Make no change

2. What is the BEST way to revise sentence 6?

   A Meet Miley Cyrus was released in 2007. It was a big success.

   B Meet Miley Cyrus was released in 2007, was a big success.

   C Meet Miley Cyrus was released in 2007 it was the big success.

   D No revision is needed.

3. Which sentence could BEST be added after sentence 11?

   A I never listened to the album.

   B It's not my favorite album.

   C I have that album.

   D It also went to #1!

Name _____ Date _____

Review

Use with Student Book pages 260–309.

Answer the questions after reading Unit 5. You can go back and reread to help find the answers.

1. In *Touching Sound with Evelyn Glennie*, what instrument did Evelyn play in New York City's Grand Central Station? Circle the letter of the correct answer.

    A marimba   **C** snare drum

    B xylophone   **D** washboard

2. "Evelyn soon found out she had what musicians call 'perfect pitch'." Perfect pitch is

    A the ability to copy notes someone else plays or sings.

    B the ability to hear notes perfectly in one's mind.

    C the ability to play any instrument without lessons.

    D the ability to perceive music in other parts of the body.

3. What do you think the film title *Touch the Sound* means?

_____

_____

4. In *A Song Map*, what is believed to be the *drinking gourd*? Circle the letter of the correct answer.

    A kind of squash   **C** the Big Dipper

    B type of ladle   **D** type of tea kettle

5. Who was Peg Leg Joe?

_____

_____

6. Use the Inference Chart below to interpret one of the verses of *Follow the Drinking Gourd*. Follow the example.

Verse	What I Know	Inference
When the sun comes back and the first quail calls...	The slaves had to cross a large river.	It was easier to cross the river in winter.

7. What was the author's purpose in writing *Austin: The Live Music Capital of the World*? Circle the letter of the correct answer.

A to entertain

B to inform

C to persuade

8. Describe in your own words why Austin is important to American music culture.

_____

_____

_____

9. What kinds of music are featured on *Austin City Limits*?

_____

_____

Home-School Connection   Tell a family member something new you learned from this unit.

Name _____ Date _____

Writing Workshop: Write a How-to Essay

Read the passage. Then read each question on the next page and circle the correct answer.

How to Plant a Tree

(1) Planting a tree is not as easy as it sounds. (2) Finally, choose the right time of year to plant. (3) The best times are fall and early spring (4) Next, choose the right place. (5) Make sure you choose a tree that grows well in your area.

(6) After you have the tree, dig a hole that is twice as wide as the root ball and add water to the hole. (7) Put the tree in the hole gentle. (8) Then cover the root ball with soil and give the tree water.

(9) Finally, put mulch around the base of the tree, and give the tree even more water. (10) Not only trees, but flowers need water. (11) You should water your tree for a few years. (12) Enjoy your tree!

1. What change, if any, should be made in sentence 2?

   A Change *Finally* to *First*

   B Change *right* to *write*

   C Change *year* to *years*

   D Make no change

2. What change, if any, should be made in sentence 3?

   A Change *times* to *time*

   B Change *are* to *is*

   C Put a period after *spring*

   D Make no change

3. What change, if any, should be made in sentence 7?

   A Change *gentle* to *gently*

   B Change *tree* to *trees*

   C Change *in* to *on*

   D Make no change

4. What is the BEST way to revise sentence 11?

   A Your tree should water for a few years.

   B You should water your tree for a few year.

   C You should your water a tree for few years.

   D No revision is needed.

5. Which sentence does NOT belong in this story?

   A Sentence 3

   B Sentence 6

   C Sentence 9

   D Sentence 10

Name _____ Date _____

Fluency

Use with Student Book page 317.

How fast are you? Use a clock. Read the text about *A Song Map*. How long did it take you? Write your time in the chart. Read three times.

A Song Map describes how one special song called "Follow the	11
Drinking Gourd" may have helped slaves escape and reach freedom.	21
The song has four stanzas, and many people think each stanza is a	34
kind of secret code that gives instructions to slaves to go north.	46
In stanza one, the song tells slaves to follow the drinking gourd, the	59
Big Dipper constellation, in the spring. If they do, an old man with a	73
wooden leg will be waiting to help them. In stanza two, slaves are	86
told to walk along the riverbank and look for marked trees to show	99
the way. Some people think the marks on the trees show a human	112
left foot and Peg Leg Joe's wooden leg. In stanza three, slaves are told	108
to look for the end of a river between two hills, with a river on the	119
other side. This may refer to Woodall Mountain in Mississippi and the	131
Tennessee River. Finally, in stanza four, the lines describe a place	142
where a great big river meets a little one. This may refer	157
to the Ohio and Tennessee Rivers.	160

My Times

189

Learning Checklist

Check off what you have learned well. Review as needed.

Word Study and Phonics

☐ Past -*ed* ending (*id, d, t*)

☐ Figurative Language

☐ Words with *ow, ou*

Strategies

☐ Identify Main Idea and Details

☐ Summarize

☐ Make Inferences

☐ Identify Author's Purpose

Grammar

☐ Subordinating Conjunctions

☐ Prepositions and Prepositional Phrases

☐ Present Perfect

Writing

☐ Problem and Solution

☐ Write a Response to Literature

☐ Write an Article about a Musician

☐ Writing Workshop: Write a How-To Essay

Listening and Speaking

☐ Listening and Speaking Workshop: Roleplay an Interview

Test Preparation

Use with Student Book pages 318–319.

Read the selection. Then answer the questions.

1 The Austin City Limits Music Festival is a three-day event in Austin, Texas. It takes place every October. People from all over the world come to play their music at the festival. People can hear all kinds of music, including country and western, bluegrass, jazz, and reggae. This is a time when many bands can celebrate their musical achievements.

2 You can bring your own water, chairs, and umbrellas to the festival. You cannot bring your own food. You can buy food and drinks there. Make sure you don't put your chair too close to the stage. Tell your parents they cannot park near the festival. It might be easier to park downtown and take a bus to the shows.

1. Why can't you bring your own food to the music festival?
  A There is food available there.
  B It is a distraction to the musicians.
  C There is no eating during performances.
  D It will cause a littering problem.

2. In paragraph I, what does <u>achievements</u> mean?
  F accomplishments
  G punishments
  H celebrations
  J compositions

3. It's better to take a bus from downtown because _____
  A you can't bring food
  B you can't park nearby
  C you can bring a chair
  D you can hear all kinds of music

Read the selection. Then answer the questions.

1 Washing your hands isn't just a good idea, it's the law for many people! All restaurants, hospitals, and many other kinds of businesses in my state must have a poster or a sign that tells their workers to wash their hands. The Department of State Health Services explains the best way to wash your hands.

2 First, get your hands wet with warm water. Put soap on your hands. Rub all parts of your hands, fingers, and thumbs with the soap. Rinse your hands to take off the soap. Then dry your hands with paper towels—the kind that the user takes out one at a time. Good hand washing is the simplest way to keep from spreading germs.

1. Hospital workers have to wash their hands because _____
   A it's the law
   B they go to restaurants
   C it's a good idea
   D there's a poster

2. The first paragraph tells _____
   F about an event
   G about a law
   H about restaurants
   J how to do something

3. The second paragraph mainly explains _____
   A why it's important for workers to wash their hands
   B how to dry your hands
   C the best way to wash your hands
   D what the Department of State Health Services does

4. Germs are _____
   F workers
   G dangerous
   H safe
   J businesses

Name _____ Date _____

Key Words

Use with Student Book pages 326–327.

| tributaries |
| national parks |
| cliffs |
| sequoias |
| grove |

A. Choose the word that *best* fits each clue. Write the word.

1. an area of land with one type of tree

   _____

2. rivers that flow into larger rivers _____

3. large trees that grow in the Northwest _____

4. parks created by a country's government

   _____

5. tall areas of rock with steep sides _____

B. Choose the word that *best* completes each sentence. Write the word.

6. The Missouri River and the Ohio River are

   _____ of the Mississippi River.

7. _____ are believed to be the tallest trees in the world.

8. It's dangerous to get too close to the edge of a

   _____ .

9. We went camping in Yellowstone, a famous

   _____ .

Academic Words

Use with Student Book page 328.

factor
participate
region

A. Choose the word that *best* completes each sentence. Write the word.

1. The height of the cliff was one _____ in his decision not to climb it.

2. Olivia loves sports, but she just doesn't have the time to _____ in them.

3. That _____ is known for being the world's largest producer of grain.

B. Match each word with its definition. Write the letter of the correct answer.

4. region   _____   **A** an area or territory

5. factor   _____   **B** a reason, element or point

6. participate _____ **C** to take part or share

C. Answer the questions.

7. Do you **participate** in any clubs? What are they?

_____

8. What **region** of the United States do you live in?

_____

9. What are some **factors** to consider when you buy a new camera?

_____

 Use each academic word in a sentence. Share your sentences with a family member.

Name _____ Date _____

Phonics: Words with *v* and *w*

Use with Student Book page 329.

Read each clue. Write the word that matches the clue. Then take turns saying the words aloud with a partner.

vacation	van	vegetables	vertical	vowels
warm	wilderness	winter	wolf	worry

1. animal related to a dog _____

2. *a, e, i, o,* and *u* are these _____

3. a small truck _____

4. a cold season _____

5. broccoli and lettuce _____

6. neither cold nor hot _____

7. time away from home or work _____

8. where the deer and the antelope live _____

9. straight up and down _____

10. think a lot about something _____

Home-School Connection Find five words that begin with the letters *v* or *w*.
Practice saying them correctly with a family member.

Comprehension: Yosemite National Park

Use with Student Book pages 330–333.

Answer the questions about the reading.

Recall

1. Why did environmentalists worry about people building in the Yosemite region?

_____

2. How many people visit Yosemite National Park each year?

_____

3. What is special about Mariposa Grove?

_____

Comprehend

4. Why shouldn't a beginner try to climb the face of El Capitan?

_____

_____

Analyze

5. How do people get to Glacier Point in winter? Why?

_____

_____

_____

Name _____ Date _____

Reader's Companion

Use with Student Book pages 330–333.

Yosemite National Park

The U.S. government stepped in to help, and in 1890, the area became known as Yosemite National Park. Rules were created to make sure the land was preserved for people to enjoy in the future. More than three million people visit the park each year.

Yosemite Valley is a popular destination for visitors. It has cliffs and rock formations, and many guests spend time gazing at its waterfalls. Yosemite Valley is open all year. People often travel to the valley by car.

Yosemite National Park is also famous for its trees. Giant sequoias seem to reach the sky. The biggest group of giant sequoias is found in Mariposa Grove. Between November and March, the road to Mariposa Grove is closed to cars because of snow. Can you think of other ways to reach the grove? You can hike or ski!

Use What You Know

List three things you might find in a national park.

1. _____

2. _____

3. _____

Genre

Underline the words in the passage that make you think this is part of a travel article.

MARK the TEXT

Reading Strategy

What connections from the article can you make to your own life?

_____

_____

_____

_____

197

Use the Strategy

How did making connections between your own life and the selection help you understand it?

_____

_____

_____

Summarize It!

Summarize the passage as if you were writing a TV commercial.

_____

_____

_____

_____

Reader's Response

Why is it important for the U.S. government to create national parks?

_____

_____

_____

Home-School Connection

Summarize the passage for a family member.

Name _____ Date _____

Learning Strategies: Make Connections

Use with Student Book pages 334–335.

Read each passage. Write about a connection you can make between each passage and your own life.

A Trip to the Museum

We have been learning about dinosaurs in school. My teacher decided to take the class to the museum to see the new dinosaur exhibit. The museum had many dinosaur bones under glass for us to look at. Scientists put together some models of dinosaur skeletons, so we could see how big the dinosaurs actually were in real life. They were huge! Some of the skeletons looked really mean. I wouldn't want to have lived in the time of the dinosaurs!

1. _____

_____

The New Book

Mrs. Milton reads to us every day after recess. She held up a new book today. The book had a large picture of the moon on it. Laura raised her hand. "Is that the moon?" she asked. "Yes," Mrs. Milton said. "This book is about the first people who landed on the moon. I was your age when I saw it on TV in 1969. What do you think it's like on the moon?" The class was excited. This is going to be a cool book!

2. _____

_____

 **Have a family member read or tell you a story. The family member can use his or her own language. Talk about how the story connects to your own life.**

Grammar: Capitalization

Use with Student Book pages 336–337.

Review the rules of **capitalization** below.

> Always capitalize **the first word of a sentence or quotation.**
> Capitalize **the first letter of a proper noun.**
> Capitalize **the first letter of most words in a title.**
> Capitalize **acronyms.**

Rewrite the sentences using proper capitalization and punctuation.

Example: i went to the top of the empire state building
<u>I went to the top of the Empire State Building.</u>

1. she can speak chinese english and french

_____

2. he used to be the director of the fbi

_____

3. her favorite book is the missing piece

_____

4. officer lopez said stop right there and turn around

_____

5. their group climbed to the top of mount everest

_____

 **Write five sentences using proper nouns. Share your ideas with a family member.**

Name _____ Date _____

Spelling: Prefixes and Suffixes

Use with Student Book pages 338–339.

Read each clue. Use the correct prefix or suffix from the chart to spell the word.

Prefixes	*re*	*dis*
Suffixes	*ful*	*ness*

> ### SPELLING TIP
>
> Learning about prefixes and suffixes will help you be a better speller. For example, the prefix *re* means "again"; *dis* means "not." The suffix *ful* means "full of," and *ness* makes a noun out of an adjective.

1. to appear again

_____

2. noun using neat

_____

3. full of power   _____

4. make again   _____

5. to not like   _____

6. noun using great   _____

7. full of color   _____

8. to not connect   _____

 Write a journal entry using at least three words that have the prefixes and suffixes above.

_____

_____

_____

 Write two new words using each prefix and suffix. Share your words with a family member.

Writing: Plan a Research Report

Fill in the charts with information to prepare for your own research report.

Choose a broad topic. Write questions and answers about the topic.

Broad Topic	
Question	
Answer	
Question	
Answer	

Write more questions to narrow down the topic. Which one do you want as your research question?

1. _____

2. _____

3. _____

Make a research plan.

What do I want to know?	Where can I find it?

Name _____ Date _____

Key Words

Use with Student Book pages 340–341.

cascade
meadow
peak
ascend
reflection
valley

A. Choose the word that _best_ fits each definition. Write the word.

1. an area of lower land between two hills or mountains _____

2. a mirror image _____

3. to move to the top of something; to go up

_____

4. a field with wild grass or flowers _____

5. the pointed top of a mountain _____

6. to flow or fall down _____

B. Choose the word that _best_ matches the meaning of the underlined words. Write the word.

7. Many different animals live in the <u>area between the two mountains</u>.

_____

8. We hoped to <u>make our way to the top of</u> the steep cliff.

_____

9. Snow covered the <u>highest point</u> of the mountain.

_____

203

Academic Words

Use with Student Book page 342.

> goal
> **highlight**
> **significant**

A. Choose the word that *best* completes each sentence. Write the word.

1. The skywriting was the _____ of the air show.

2. There were a few _____ problems in their plan.

3. Even though he set his _____ very high, he was able to achieve it.

B. Choose the word that best matches the meaning of the underlined words. Write the word.

4. The soldier's <u>aim</u> was to return the flag to camp.

_____

5. Protecting the animals was the <u>important</u> factor in his decision.

_____

6. The <u>most memorable</u> part of the show was the Arabian dance.

_____

C. Answer the questions.

7. What was the **highlight** of the last school year for you?

_____

8. What are your **goals** for the future?

_____

 **Use each academic word in a sentence. Share your sentences with a family member.**

Name _____ Date _____

Word Study: Greek and Latin Word Roots

Use with Student Book page 343.

Latin Roots	Greek Roots
sub: under	*log*: speech
vac: to empty	*path*: feeling, suffering
cele: to honor	*scope*: to see
vis: to look	*phon*: sound

Read each sentence. Write the Greek or Latin word root that each underlined word comes from. The first one is done for you.

1. A <u>submarine</u> can travel deep below the sea.

_____ sub _____

2. Air is <u>invisible</u>. _____

3. I felt a lot of <u>sympathy</u> for the sick kitten. _____

4. Did you hear the <u>telephone</u> ring? _____

5. The actors had a lot of <u>dialogue</u> to learn. _____

6. You can see Mars with a <u>telescope</u>. _____

7. We like to <u>celebrate</u> on holidays. _____

8. I <u>vacuum</u> the rug every morning to get it clean.

_____

Find five more words with Greek or Latin word roots. Show your words to a family member.

Comprehension: My Trip to Yosemite

Use with Student Book pages 344–347.

Answer the questions about the reading.

Recall

1. What was Jay's goal on the first day of the trip?

____

2. How does Jay feel about rock climbing?

____

3. Why was Jay sore after the mule ride?

____

Comprehend

4. What was the difference between Jay's August 8 and August 9 entries?

____

____

Analyze

5. What do you think will happen when Mirror Lake turns into a meadow?

____

____

____

Name _____ Date _____

Reader's Companion

Use with Student Book pages 344–347.

My Trip to Yosemite

August 7

On our first day, we drove to Glacier Point. Our goal was to ascend to the very top. We had a great view from there and saw the huge Yosemite Falls. We could see Yosemite Valley at the bottom. There were so many trees in the valley! We saw Half Dome mountain. It looks like the top of a circle. We passed rock climbers on the way down. People come from all over the world to climb rocks in Yosemite. It looked fun, but also a little scary!

Use What You Know

List three things you saw at a place you visited.

1. _____

2. _____

3. _____

Comprehension Check MARK the TEXT

What is the author describing? Underline the words that helped you find your answer.

_____

_____

_____

_____

Reading Strategy MARK the TEXT

Review the passage with a partner. Circle the words you would use to summarize the passage to a partner.

Use the Strategy

How did reviewing and retelling help you to understand the selection?

_____

_____

_____

Summarize It!

Summarize the passage as if you were writing a story about Jay's trip.

_____

_____

_____

_____

Reader's Response

Would you like to go rock climbing? Why or why not?

_____

_____

_____

Copyright © by Pearson Education, Inc.

Summarize the passage for a family member.

Name _____ Date _____

Learning Strategies: Review and Retell

Use with Student Book pages 348–349.

Read the passage. Answer the questions.

An Island Adventure

Dad and I were stuck on an island. The island was out in the middle of the bay, not far from our house. We had been fishing offshore. Suddenly, it started getting windy. The sail ripped. "Let's pull the boat to shore," said Dad. Together, we pulled our small sailboat onto the sand. We sat and waited. We waited a bit longer. "I'm sure someone will come and find us," said Dad. "Don't worry," I said. "I left Mom a note. I told her we would be fishing near the island." Dad started to laugh. "You're very smart, Chelsea!" Within an hour, we saw Mom racing to the shore in our little speedboat. We were glad to see her. She brought lunch!

1. Why did Chelsea and her dad have to bring their boat ashore?

_____

_____

2. Why wasn't Chelsea worried about being stuck on the beach?

_____

_____

3. Why were Chelsea and her dad happy to see Mom?

_____

_____

 Have a family member read or tell you a story. The family member can use his or her own language. Retell the story to another family member.

Grammar: Active and Passive Voice

Use with Student Book pages 350–351.

Review the difference between the **active and the passive voice.**

Active	A truck hit the car. A woman planted the flowers.
Passive	The car was hit by a truck. The flowers were planted by a woman.

Rewrite each active voice sentence to make it passive voice.

Example: That famous singer performed a concert.
 <u>A concert was performed by that famous singer.</u>

1. The teacher called on the boy.

_____

2. Vanesa wrote the article.

_____

3. Musicians in the United States created country western music.

_____

4. The police finally caught the thief.

_____

5. My mother baked the chocolate cake.

_____

 **Write five sentences in the active voice. Then change them to the passive voice. Share your ideas with a family member.**

Name _____ Date _____

Spelling: Words That Are Difficult to Spell

Use with Student Book pages 352–353.

Find the word in each sentence that is spelled incorrectly. Spell the word correctly.

1. Every place on Earth is part of an ecosistem.

_____

2. Konservation work will save the

environment. _____

3. All of the smaller tributarys flowed into the big river.

_____

4. It took the climbers three days to reach the mowntain peak.

_____

5. We live on the edge of a national forrest. _____

6. We had fun rowwing our boat on the lake.

_____

 Write a paragraph using at least three words that you have had trouble spelling.

_____

_____

_____

 **Write the dictionary definitions to three words you have trouble spelling. Show your work to a family member.**

Writing: Paraphrasing a Source

Fill in the charts with information to prepare for your own research report.

Choose two paragraphs from one or more of your sources. Express the ideas in your own words. Then list the citation for paraphrase.

Text from Source	Paraphrase	Citation

Text from Source	Paraphrase	Citation

Name _____ Date _____

Key Words

Use with Student Book pages 354–355.

campsite
formation
incline
ranger station
rescue
encounter

A. Choose the word that *best* completes each sentence. Write the word.

1. You might _____ wild bears if you camp in the American Northwest.

2. There is an interesting rock _____ on the top of that hill.

3. That may look like a small hill, but the _____ is quite steep.

4. Bears ate all the food at our _____ while we were asleep.

5. The _____ is the best place to go if you need help when you are camping.

6. The rangers had to _____ the rock climber who fell.

B. Write TRUE or FALSE.

7. If you rescue someone, you do not help. _____

8. If you encounter a wild animal, you see or meet an animal. _____

9. You are on an incline when you come down a hill. _____

10. Most people have a campsite inside their house. _____

11. Some formations are made of rock. _____

Academic Words

Use with Student Book page 356.

> exhibit
> injured
> deduce

A. **Choose the word that *best* completes each sentence. Write the word.**

1. Scientists say that many animals _____ intelligence.

2. It did not take long for the detective to _____ the motive for the robbery.

3. The athlete _____ his knee, but doctors say he will recover.

B. **Choose the word that best matches the meaning of the underlined words. Write the word.**

4. The girl's arm was <u>broken</u> during the accident.

   _____

5. He <u>figured out</u> the answer to the puzzle easily.

   _____

6. Dogs <u>show</u> fear by putting their tails between their legs.

   _____

C. **Answer the questions.**

7. How do you **exhibit** fear?

   _____

8. Have you ever been **injured**? How?

   _____

 **Use each academic word in a sentence. Share your sentences with a family member.**

Name _____ Date _____

Phonics: Variant Vowel *oo*

Use with Student Book page 357.

Read each sentence. Underline the *oo* words that have the sound you hear in *took*. Draw a box around the *oo* words that have the sound you hear in *too*. The first one is done for you.

1. Have people ever <u>stood</u> on the moon?

2. I learned how to cook in school.

3. The wind took the roof off our house.

4. Bamboo and oak are two kinds of wood.

5. A cool breeze feels good on a hot day!

6. The book was full of Mother Goose rhymes.

7. There is a zoo in the neighborhood.

8. Here's a cool picture of the fish I didn't hook.

9. Don't be gloomy. Things will look better tomorrow.

10. My sister took the shampoo!

11. Don't forget to bring your notebook to our classroom.

12. My little sister left her book in my bedroom.

Think of five more words with variant sound /oo/. Show your words to a family member.

215

Comprehension: A Night at Great Basin

Use with Student Book pages 358–365.

Answer the questions about the reading.

Recall

1. Why did the father buy new boots for his sons but not for himself?

_____

2. How did the boys' father injure his leg on the trail?

_____

3. What are javelinas?

_____

Comprehend

4. Why didn't Miguel ask his father what he meant by trouble?

_____

_____

Analyze

5. What do you think the relationship was like between the boys' father and their grandfather?

_____

_____

_____

Name _____ Date _____

Reader's Companion

Use with Student Book pages 358–365.

A Night at Great Basin

"Hey Dad," observed Miguel, "you bought Luis and me new boots for this trip, but yours are falling apart."

"Those are my lucky boots, from hikes I took as a teenager with your grandfather," his father answered, adding affectionately, "Luis, come help me snap these tent poles together."

When the tent was erected, their father showed the boys a book he had brought along: *Wildlife of Great Basin.* "There are scorpions here, but humans rarely see them. There are also bobcats and mountain lions, but most park visitors never see them either."

Use What You Know

List three wild animals that can be found at Great Basin.

1. _____

2. _____

3. _____

Comprehension Check

MARK the TEXT

Underline the name of the book the boys' dad brought with him.

Reading Strategy

MARK the TEXT

Why does their dad wear his old boots? Circle the text where you found your answer.

_____

_____

_____

Use the Strategy

How did drawing conclusions help you understand the passage?

_____

_____

_____

Summarize It!

Summarize the passage as if you were Miguel.

_____

_____

_____

_____

Reader's Response

What animals would you like to see in the wild? Why?

_____

_____

_____

Summarize the passage for a family member.

Learning Strategies: Draw Conclusions

Use with Student Book pages 366–367.

Read the passage. Answer the questions.

The View

"Look over there," said Marilee. "You can see the whole town!" Buddy quickly turned his head. He could see Main Street and their school. "Look over there," said Buddy, as the wind blew off his baseball cap. "You can see the little island where we go camping every summer." Marilee and Buddy were having a great time. "Too bad we have to go soon," said Marilee. Buddy smiled. "I know," he said. "Mom wants us home at five o'clock."

1. Where are Marilee and Buddy?

_____ **A** in an airplane

_____ **B** on the side of a hill

_____ **C** in their backyard

2. Explain why you chose your answer. Explain why you didn't choose the other two answers.

_____

_____

_____

3. Do Marilee and Buddy want to go home? Why or why not?

_____

_____

Have a family member read or tell you a story. The family member can use his or her own language. Talk about what conclusions you can draw from the story.

Grammar:
Italics, Underlining, and Quotation Marks

Use with Student Book pages 368–369.

Review these simple rules about italics, underlining, and quotation marks.

Rewrite each sentence using correct italics, underlining, or quotation marks.

> Use *italics* or <u>underlining</u> for:
> - **titles of books, plays, newspapers, magazines, movies, TV shows, and CDs;**
> - **foreign words** not common in English; and
> - **emphasis.**
>
> Use **quotation marks** for titles of **short stories, songs,** and **poems.**

Example: I always watch American Idol on TV.
> I always watch <u>American Idol</u> on TV.

1. Have you ever seen the movie Marley and Me?

   _____

2. I am reading Charlie and the Chocolate factory now.

   _____

3. She tried on a kimono when she visited Japan.

   _____

4. You must not chew gum during an interview.

   _____

5. She cried when she heard the song The Rose.

   _____

 **Write five sentences using italics, underlining, or quotations. Share your ideas with a family member.**

Name _____ Date _____

Spelling:

Checking Your Spelling

Use with Student Book pages 370–371.

Write the correct word to complete each sentence.

SPELLING TIP

You can use your computer's spell check to check your spelling, but the computer can't tell whether you meant *weather* or *whether*, or *your* or *you're*. You must still check your spelling carefully.

1. Andy wanted an apple,

_____ .
    (to   too   two)

2. _____ the best player on the team.
    (Your   You're)

3. I would like to pass my art _____ .
    (coarse   course)

4. I _____ your invitation to the party.
    (accept   except)

5. I put my _____ on when I get dressed.
    (close   clothes)

6. The head of the school is the _____ .
    (principle   principal)

Write a paragraph using at least three words that can be mistaken for other words.

_____

_____

Find five more words that you confuse with other words. Look up each word in the dictionary and use it in a sentence. Show your work to a family member.

Writing: Quoting a Source

Fill in the charts with information to prepare for your own research report.

Choose two quotations you would like to use in your report. Fill in the charts. List the citation for the quotations.

Information Search	Direct Quote	Citation

Information Search	Direct Quote	Citation

Name _____ Date _____

Review
Use with Student Book pages 320–371.

Answer the questions after reading Unit 6. You can go back and reread to help find the answers.

1. According to *Yosemite National Park*, how long have people lived in the Yosemite region? Circle the letter of the correct answer.
   A 50 years   **C** 100 years
   B 8,000 years   **D** 500 years

2. Why did the government create Yosemite National Park?

   _____

   _____

3. Why is it dangerous to climb El Capitan?

   _____

   _____

4. According to *My Trip to Yosemite*, which waterfall is the tallest waterfall in the United States? Circle the letter of the correct answer.
   A Niagara Falls   **C** Yosemite Falls
   B Vernal Falls   **D** Nevada Falls

5. Name three places Jay and his family visited.

   _____

   _____

6. What did Jay learn about Mirror Lake on his mule ride?

   _____

   _____

7. What phrase has the same meaning as *encounter*? Circle the correct answer.

  A help someone in trouble   **C** come into contact with
  B a place with a tent for sleeping   **D** a group of objects

8. What kinds of wildlife did the boys' father say could be found in Great Basin?

_____

_____

9. In *A Night at Great Basin*, do you think the father's boots were lucky? Why or why not?

_____

_____

Home-School Connection Tell a family member something new you learned in this unit.

224

Name _____ Date _____

Writing Workshop: Write a Research Report

Read the passage. Then read each question on the next page and circle the correct answer.

Pluto's Fame

(1) Pluto was discovered on 1930. (2) At that time it was called the ninth planet in our solar system. (3) However, in 2006, the International Astronomical Union (IAU) said Pluto is not a planet. (4) The IAU main office is in France. (5) Now it is called a "dwarf planet."

(6) The discovery of Pluto was important news in 1930. (7) People suggested more than 1,000 names for the new planet. (8) The name "Pluto" came from an 11-year-old girl in England.

(9) Since then, Pluto gave its name to two other things. (10) One is the cartoon character Pluto, which was created in 1930 by Disney. (11) The other is "plutonium," an element created in 1940.

(12) Many scientists do not agree with the IAU's decision. (13) On the other hand, many people still call Pluto "the ninth planet."

1 What change, if any, should be made in sentence 1?

  A Change *on* to *in*

  B Change *was* to *is*

  C Change *discovered* to *discover*

  D Make no change

2 What is the BEST way to revise sentence 7?

  A People suggested 1,000 more than names for the new planet.

  B People suggested more than 1,000 names for the new planet.

  C People suggested more than 1,000 for the new planet names.

  D No revision is needed.

3 What change, if any, should be made in sentence 9?

  A Change *its* to *it's*

  B Change *things* to *thing*

  C Change *other* to *others*

  D Make no change

4 What change, if any, should be made in sentence 13?

  A Change *On the other hand* to *As a result*

  B Change *call* to *calls*

  C Change *on* to *in*

  D Make no change

5 Which sentence does NOT belong in this story?

  A Sentence 2

  B Sentence 4

  C Sentence 9

  D Sentence 12

Name _____ Date _____

Fluency

Use with Student Book page 381.

How fast are you? Use a clock. Read the text about *My Trip to Yosemite*. How long did it take you? Write your time in the chart. Read three times.

My Trip to Yosemite is part of a scrapbook in which Jay describes	13
a trip he and his family took to the national park in the month of	28
August. They camped out in a tent and visited different sights in the	41
park each day. The first day, the family drove to the top of Glacier	55
Point. They had a great view from there, and saw a huge waterfall,	68
the trees in Yosemite Valley at the bottom, and Half Dome Mountain.	80
They also saw rock climbers. On the second day, they rode mules	92
through Yosemite Valley. Jay saw Mirror Lake, and learned it was	103
slowly turning into a meadow. The family went to the Merced River	115
to swim and watch people go rafting. The next day, everyone wanted	127
to see some of the beautiful waterfalls. Jay took a tour of Vernal Falls	141
and Nevada Falls. He also saw the huge, very old sequoia trees in	154
Mariposa Grove. What a great vacation!	160

My Times

Learning Checklist

Check off what you have learned well. Review as needed.

Word Study and Phonics

☐ Words with *v* and *w*

☐ Greek and Latin Word Roots

☐ Variant vowel (*oo*)

Strategies

☐ Make Connections

☐ Review and Retell

☐ Draw Conclusions

Grammar

☐ Capitalization

☐ Active and Passive Voice

☐ Italics, Underlining, and Quotation Marks

Writing

☐ Plan a Research Report

☐ Paraphrasing a Source

☐ Quoting a Source

☐ Writing Workshop: Write a Research Report

Listening and Speaking

☐ Listening and Speaking Workshop: Present a TV Commercial

Name _____ Date _____

Test Preparation

Use with Student Book pages 382–383.

Read the selection. Then choose the correct words to fill in the blanks.

1 How did the hot springs in Big Bend National Park form? If you could ___1___ down through the Earth's crust, you would see that the rocks in the crust get ___2___ the further down you go. The water that is near or touching the hot rocks also gets hot and comes up to the surface. When the water does this, it becomes a hot spring.

2 In areas near volcanoes, like in Yellowstone National Park, the water comes in contact with molten rock called magma. The water that touches magma becomes so hot it ___3___. Steam rises above Earth's crust in the form of a geyser. Old Faithful is one of the most famous ___4___ in the world!

1
A hear
B travel
C swim
D meet

2
F heavier
G lighter
H hotter
J colder

3
A boils
B flows
C freezes
D melts

4
F waterfalls
G hot springs
H earthquakes
J geysers

Read the selection. Then choose the correct words to fill in the blanks.

The bald eagle is the only eagle that can only be found in ___1___. It lives in many places between Alaska and northern Mexico. Adult males have ___2___ that are 6 1/2 feet from one end to the other. The female bald eagles are even ___3___. Their wings are about 8 feet from one end to the other. Eagles live for 30 years or more. Eagles choose one mate for their whole life. A ___4___ of eagles builds its nest in a big tree near a river or lake. They add new material to their nest each year, so some nests may weigh up to 2,000 pounds. Bald eagles eat mostly fish and birds.

1

   A Europe

   B Antarctica

   C North America

   D South America

2

   F heads

   G beaks

   H wings

   J feet

3

   A bigger

   B smaller

   C fatter

   D faster

4

   F team

   G population

   H group

   J pair